Andrew Linn
Cambridge 1994

CAMBRIDGE STUDIES IN LINGUISTICS

General Editors: B. COMRIE, C. J. FILLMORE, R. LASS, R. B. LE PAGE,
J. LYONS, P. H. MATTHEWS, F. R. PALMER, R. POSNER, S. ROMAINE,
N. V. SMITH, J. L. M. TRIM, A. ZWICKY

Syntactic theory in the High Middle Ages

In this series

Supplementary Volumes

* Issued in hard covers and as a paperback

SYNTACTIC THEORY IN THE HIGH MIDDLE AGES

Modistic models of sentence structure

MICHAEL A. COVINGTON

Research Associate
Office of Computing and Information Services
University of Georgia

The right of the
University of Cambridge
to print and sell
all manner of books
was granted by
Henry VIII in 1534.
The University has printed
and published continuously
since 1584.

CAMBRIDGE UNIVERSITY PRESS

CAMBRIDGE

LONDON   NEW YORK   NEW ROCHELLE

MELBOURNE   SYDNEY

Published by the Press Syndicate of the University of Cambridge
The Pitt Building, Trumpington Street, Cambridge CB2 1RP
32 East 57th Street, New York, NY 10022, USA
296 Beaconsfield Parade, Middle Park, Melbourne 3206, Australia

First published 1984

Printed in Great Britain by Antony Rowe Ltd., Chippenham

Library of Congress catalogue card number: 84–5799

British Library Cataloguing in Publication Data
Covington, Michael A.
Syntactic theory in the High Middle Ages.
– (Cambridge studies in linguistics,
ISSN 0068–676X; 39)
1. Grammar, comparative and general – Syntax
2. Linguistics – History
I. Title
415   P291
ISBN 0 521 25679 8

AO

Contents

SOLI DEO GLORIA

Preface

This book is a revised version of a Ph.D. dissertation written at Yale under the direction of Rulon Wells, to whom I shall always be grateful for showing me the value, and beginning to teach me the art, of asking interesting questions about anything and everything.

It must also serve as a memorial to the late Professor Jan Pinborg, Director of the Institute of Medieval Greek and Latin Philology at the University of Copenhagen, who took a great interest in it and provided me with much help while it was being written, but unfortunately did not live to see it published. His last communication to me, just a few weeks before he died, was a detailed set of comments on my dissertation; they were invaluable in preparing the present version.

This work would not have been possible without the aid of National Science Foundation Grant Number BNS-81-05359, which enabled me to travel to Europe, examine manuscripts, confer with scholars, and assemble a microfilm collection. Many people offered assistance and advice along the way; some who deserve special thanks are R. H. Robins (University of London), Bruce Barker-Benfield (Oxford), W. Keith Percival (Kansas), Irène Rosier (CNRS, France), C. H. Kneepkens (Nijmegen), K. M. Fredborg (Copenhagen); the two additional readers of the original dissertation at Yale, Edward Stankiewicz and C. J. Herington; and P. H. Matthews, who served as reader for the Cambridge University Press. All conclusions and opinions expressed here are of course my own and do not necessarily reflect the views of any of the people acknowledged here, nor of the National Science Foundation or any other governmental agency.

Finally, heartfelt thanks are surely due to my wife Melody for encouragement, endurance, and moral support, and to my mother, Hazel R. Covington, for whom my Ph.D. thesis marked the culmination of many years of hard work and sacrifice undertaken in an effort to give me the best education possible.

Los Angeles, California
17 August 1983

1 Introduction

The speculative grammarians of the High Middle Ages are remembered today for two major achievements; they formulated the theory of *modi significandi*, which comprises an elaborate attempt to explain linguistic structure in terms of the structure of cognition and of reality, and they developed an elaborate theory of syntax from which some concepts, such as government and dependency, have survived to the present day. The former has been studied extensively in modern times, while the latter has been neglected.

This book deals with the origins and development of the theories of syntactic structure used by a group of grammarians and logicians who flourished at Paris between about 1270 and 1310 and who were later called 'Modistae' because of their emphasis on *modi significandi*. I am focusing on roughly the period from Martin of Dacia (c. 1270), who was, as far as we know, the first to construct a fully modistic theory of syntax, to Radulphus Brito (c. 1300), the last major contributor to modistic theory before the rise of nominalism diverted grammarians' attention to methodological matters.

The primary goal of my study is exegesis. I am concerned more with explicating the conceptual content of the medieval theory than with presenting its complete history. In so doing, I am consciously writing for two audiences – linguists who may know little about medieval philosophy, and medievalists who may know little about linguistics – and I hope readers in each group will forgive me for having done certain things purely for the benefit of the other. Linguists wanting to know more about medieval thought should look at books such as Lindberg (1978) and Lewis (1964) (which is of much more general relevance than its title suggests); medievalists may want to consult Matthews (1981) on points of linguistics. Moreover, two important reference works – Bursill-Hall's *Census of Medieval Latin Grammatical Manuscripts* (1981) and the *Cambridge History of Later Medieval Philosophy* (1982) – have been published since most of this book was written; they are now indispensable for any further work in the field.

Many of my sources are available in printed editions, though I have consulted manuscripts where appropriate. I have standardized the orthography in all Latin quotations; to do otherwise would have added nothing and would have made proofreading nearly impossible. Also, I have made occasional changes in punctuation, though not such as to alter the clause structure. I have indicated emendations to printed texts by means of square brackets (for interpolated comments) or angle brackets (for short insertions).

I have given all important Latin quotations in parallel columns of text and translation, both to increase the usefulness of this work to non-Latinists and as a way of presenting my interpretations of difficult passages. Medieval scientific Latin has many words and phrases, such as *item* and *dicendum est*, which mark the exact position of the sentence in the highly structured discourse from which it is taken; I have generally left these in place on the Latin side but have not attempted to render them into English, since there is no way to do so concisely.

Moreover, most theoretical terms in medieval grammar have no counterparts in modern languages. Many of them I have simply calqued (*modus significandi*: 'mode of signifying', *constructibile*: 'constructible') or left in Latin (*regimen, primum, secundum*). Translating into modern terminology (e.g., rendering *causa inventionis* as 'functional explanation' and *partes orationis* as 'components of the sentence') can be useful in restricted contexts but, if followed as a general practice, would tend to exaggerate the similarities between medieval and modern theories – or, worse, make it impossible to separate the medieval doctrines from my tentative interpretations of them.

Although comparison of medieval and modern theories is not among my main goals, I have not hesitated to introduce insights from modern grammatical theories where appropriate (particularly in Chapter 5). In this connection one must avoid two opposite errors. On the one hand, to study past linguistic theories 'in and of themselves,' as is sometimes advocated, would be to ignore the fact that linguistics, unlike art or literature, is the scientific investigation of a natural phenomenon – language – and hence that many of the properties of linguistic theories, past and present, result from the properties of the thing being studied, not just the creativity of the theorizers. No one would study medieval astronomy without looking at modern analyses of planetary motion; it would make equally little sense to study medieval grammar without looking at the best grammatical analyses available today.

On the other hand, it would be just as much a mistake to assume that the Modistae are interesting only because, and insofar as, they anticipated modern developments. No one who is familiar with both can doubt that some of the issues faced by medieval and modern syntacticians are similar – for instance, the constituency-dependency question discussed in sections 5.1 and 5.2 – but the medieval philosophical environment and (even more so) the overall medieval frame of mind are very different from those of the present day; indeed, it is the difference as much as the similarity that makes the Modistae interesting. (The discovery of Pāṇini by the West was, after all, far more exciting than the discovery of a precursor of Locke or Turgot would have been.) In the final analysis, the history of linguistics, like any field of knowledge that is speculative in the Aristotelian sense, needs no external justification; like Mount Everest, it is of interest simply 'because it's there.'

2 Before the Modistae

Modistic syntactic theory represents in large part the continued development of earlier ideas. Its background begins with the late Roman grammarians who wrote down descriptions of the classical Latin language for posterity – writers such as Donatus, Charisius, Diomedes, and Servius in the fourth century, Phocas and Pompeius in the fifth, and Priscian in the early sixth. The grammarians of the Carolingian Renaissance, such as Alcuin of York (fl. 781–96), Sedulius Scottus (fl. 848–58), and Remigius of Auxerre (c. 900), made use of the writings of many of their Roman predecessors and kept essentially the same descriptive framework.

By the eleventh or twelfth century, however, the range of Roman grammarians whose works were used in the schools of northern Europe had narrowed to two: Donatus and Priscian. The *Ars grammatica* of Donatus – the first part of which, the *Ars minor*, is phrased in a catechism-like question-and-answer format – says nothing significant about syntax. The only substantial Roman source for medieval syntactic theory is therefore Priscian, whose eighteen-book *Institutiones grammaticae* constitute the most voluminous, most thorough, and most disorganized of the surviving Roman grammars. The first sixteen books, referred to in the Middle Ages as *Priscianus maior*, discuss the individual parts of speech, and the last two (*Priscianus minor*) are explicitly devoted to syntax, though syntactic information is scattered through the other books as well.

Priscian's stated goal (*Institutiones* I.1) is to pass along to the Romans the insights of various Greek grammarians, especially Apollonius Dyscolus, and his treatment of syntax is heavily dependent on Apollonius' Περὶ Συντάξεως (*On Syntax*); but since Priscian's Greek antecedents were not known to the medieval Latin grammarians with whom I am concerned, I shall not try to trace them exhaustively. On the whole, Priscian is far less theory-oriented than the Modistae; his brief discussions of general principles tend (even more than those of Apollonius) to be followed by long enumerations of examples from classical literature, cited either because they illustrate important points or, more commonly, because they present minor problems and therefore need explaining.

2.1 Priscian on syntax

For Priscian, the number of parts of speech (*partes orationis*, more literally 'parts of the sentence' or 'sentence components') is a fundamental theoretical issue. He argues that there are eight: noun, verb, participle, pronoun, preposition, adverb, conjunction, and interjection (II.15–21). For him, 'noun' comprises both substantives and adjectives; interrogatives and relatives like *quis*, 'who?' and *qui*, 'who, which' are nouns, not pronouns; and 'preposition' includes both separate words and prefixes. His criteria for identifying the parts of speech involve a haphazard mix of semantic, syntactic, and morphological criteria. For example:

Proprium est nominis substantiam et qualitatem significare. (II.18)	The distinguishing characteristic of the noun is that it signifies substance and quality.
Proprium est verbi actionem sive passionem sive utrumque cum modis et formis et temporibus sine casu significare. (II.20)	The distinguishing characteristic of the verb is that it signifies action, or the undergoing of action, or either of the two indifferently, with moods and inflections [for person] and tenses, without case.
Proprium est adverbii cum verbo poni nec sine eo perfectam significationem posse habere. (II.20)	The distinguishing characteristic of the adverb is that it is put with the verb and can have no complete meaning without it.
Proprium est coniunctionis diversa nomina vel quascumque dictiones casuales vel diversa verba vel adverbia coniungere. (II.21)	The distinguishing characteristic of the conjunction is that it joins different nouns, or any kind of words inflected for case, or verbs, or adverbs.

Priscian holds that, like the letters of the alphabet, the parts of speech form not merely a closed set but an ordered set – in fact, the same is true of the sets of cases, genders, tenses, and so forth (XVII.12).[1] He argues that the *ordo naturalis* of the parts of speech is:

NOUN > VERB > PARTICIPLE > PRONOUN >
PREPOSITION > ADVERB > CONJUNCTION > INTERJECTION

(By '>' here I mean 'precedes' or 'is prior to'.)

The rationale for this ordering is as follows. The noun and verb come at the beginning because they alone have to be present (at least implicitly) in every sentence (XVII.12–13). The noun is prior to the verb because substance (signified by nouns) is ontologically prior to action (signified by verbs) (XVII.14). The participle is obviously next in line because of its close relationship with, and dependence on, the verb (XVII.18–19). Then comes the pronoun, which would have been next to the noun if its position had not been preempted by the verb and the participle. Those are the inflected parts of speech; they are, as a class, prior to the uninflected parts of speech (*indeclinabilia*). Of the latter, the preposition comes first (Priscian does not really say why); then the adverb (because it modifies, and thus corresponds to, the verb, which is second in the order as a whole); then the conjunction, because it can join words from any of the categories that precede it and is therefore dependent on all of them; and, last of all, the interjection (XVII.20).[2]

At first sight it might seem that Priscian's *ordo naturalis* has to do with word order, but this is not so; the relation of *ordo naturalis* holding between one part of speech and another can be the opposite of the normal word order. For instance, in the sentence the preposition (whether functioning as a separate word or as a prefix) always precedes the inflected part of speech to which it is attached; but it comes after the inflected parts of speech in the *ordo naturalis*. 'Ergo natura quidem posterior est, constructione vero principalis' (XVII.20) – the preposition is subsequent by nature but initial in the construction.

Priscian's theory of syntactic structure, insofar as he has one, is elegantly simple. Phonological segments (*litterae*, or more properly *elementa*) go together to form syllables (*syllabae*); syllables make up words (*dictiones*); and words are put together to form sentences (*orationes*). Each of these four primitive units is independently definable: the segment is the shortest unit into which speech can be divided (I.3), the syllable is what is pronounced with one accent[3] and one breath (II.1), the word is the shortest unit that has meaning out of context (II.14), and the sentence is 'a grammatical sequence of words, manifesting a complete thought' ('ordinatio dictionum congrua, sententiam perfectam demonstrans,' II.53).

The four primitive units, segment, syllable, word, and sentence, are related by three levels of distributional constraints, which Priscian considers to be parallel in nature. To take some of his examples, the segment *h* occurs only at the beginning of the syllable; the syllable *prae* occurs only at the beginning of the word;[4] and a particular class of words, the prepositions, always come before the words to which they are joined (XVII.7). (Priscian's exposition becomes unclear at this point; another, better example, which he hints at but does not state clearly, is the fact that relative pronouns and subordinating conjunctions always come at the beginning of the clause.) The *partes orationis* (literally 'sentence components', not 'parts of speech') are to the sentence what vowels and consonants are to the syllable: classes of constituents (XVII.10).

All of this leaves out morphology, which Priscian handles with what Hockett (1954) and Robins (1959) classify as a 'word-and-paradigm' model: inflection is a kind of variation that whole words undergo, rather than a matter of selecting and attaching appropriate affixes. For Priscian, *puella* is the nominative of 'girl' and *puellae* is the genitive of the same word; he would never say that *puell-* is 'girl' and *-ae* is genitive. An analogue to this in modern theory is the representation of inflectional categories as features attached to lexical items, rather than as separate elements in the string of morphemes.

Priscian does not go very far toward his goal of treating sentence syntax and phonology in parallel fashion because his method of stating distributional constraints in terms of linear order, which works so well for describing the behavior of segments and syllables, is rather poorly suited to handling sentence structure. Latin has highly variable word order and indicates grammatical relations mainly by means of case endings, not linear position; yet Priscian's distributionalism keeps him from saying anything more about grammatical relations than that one word 'is put in construction with' (*construitur cum*) or 'requires' (*exigit*) another. He makes no attempt to define grammatical relations precisely; even the concepts of subject and object (as distinct from the cases that mark them) are absent. It is hardly surprising that Priscian's idea of parallel syntax and phonology was completely rejected by the Modistae.

On a more *ad hoc* level, however, Priscian formulated (or passed on from Apollonius) a number of syntactic concepts that were to be influential in the Middle Ages. Percival (to appear) notes that Priscian has at least the germ of a concept of morphological government – the notion that one word is responsible for the case or mood of another – though he has no technical term for it. Further, Priscian often appeals, in an informal way, to the idea that certain parts of the sentence are understood (*subaudiuntur*, (*sub*)*intelleguntur*) or left out (*per figuram* ἐλλείψεως); for example, when the infinitive *gaudere* is used as an imperative, *iubeo*, 'I bid you to ...' is understood with it (XVIII.48), and in *non bonus homo* 'not a good man', the adverb *non* only seems to modify a noun; in reality it modifies an understood verb *est* (II.20). In one place (XVIII.10) he proposes a rule for interpreting possessives by paraphrasing them; in his example, *Hector filius Priami*, 'Hector son of Priam', is converted to *Hectorem filium Priamus possidet*, 'Priam possesses a son, Hector'.

Moreover, Priscian promotes the concept of *transitio personarum* – the transfer of the action from one person or referent to another.[5] In a transitive sentence, such as *Aristophanes Aristarchum docuit*, 'Aristophanes taught Aristarchus', the action (in this case teaching) proceeds from Aristophanes to Aristarchus (XIII.23). If there is no transfer of action, as in *percurrit homo excelsus*, 'an eminent man finishes the course',[6] then the sentence or construction is said to be intransitive (XIV.14), and if the action is transferred back to the person from which it came, as in *Aiax se interfecit*, 'Ajax killed himself', the construction is described as reciprocal (XIII.23). A retransitive construction is one in which the action goes from one person to another and then back to the first, as in *orare iussit ... ut ad se venias*, 'He₁ commanded (me₂) to ask (you₃) to come to him₁,' (XIV.14, indicating the various referents with subscript numbers for clarity). Percival (to appear) observes that 'it would not appear that Priscian regarded this classification as exhaustive,' but much was made of it during the Middle Ages.

2.2 The reunion of grammar and logic

Beginning late in the tenth century, the study of logic, which had been languishing for about four centuries, underwent an important revival. The last great logician of antiquity had been Boethius (roughly contemporary with Priscian), whose works, including translations of Aristotle's *Categories* and *De interpretatione* and Porphyry's *Isagoge*, remained available (though neglected) during the succeeding centuries. After Boethius, one elementary treatise on logic was written (c. 778) by Alcuin of

York, but logic did not become the object of intensive scholarly research until the time of Gerbert of Aurillac (938?–1003), 'the first man in Europe, so far as we know, to lecture systematically on the whole range of Boethius' logical treatises' (Southern 1953 · 175). There is doubtless no way to tell to what extent Gerbert himself was responsible, but there certainly ensued a sharp rise in scholars' interest in logic, continuing through the halting first steps of Garlandus Compotista (fl. c. 1040) and Anselm of Canterbury (1033–1109) up to Peter Abelard (1079–1142), the first great medieval logician – by which time the remaining works of Aristotle were being rediscovered and the rise of scholasticism was well under way.

With the revival of logic came a restoration of the link between logic and grammar that had existed in Stoic times but had been broken long before the time of Priscian. Heretofore, Latin writers had confined themselves either to grammar or to logic, and even those who wrote about both, such as Alcuin, made no attempt to relate the two fields (de Rijk 1967a:98–9). The re-establishment of the connection resulted in a period of rapid progress in both fields, about which little is known (see, however, Hunt 1943); for grammar this culminated in the Priscian commentaries of William of Conches (first edition c. 1125, second c. 1150) and his pupil Petrus Helias (c. 1140). William of Conches was forgotten all too soon, but Petrus Helias' work was well known throughout the Middle Ages and was used extensively by the Modistae.

The nature of twelfth-century philosophical grammar is manifest in William of Conches's famous plaint, at the end of his *De philosophia mundi*:[7]

Priscianus ... obscuras dat definitiones nec exponit, causas vero inventionis diversarum partium et diversorum accidentium in unaquaque praetermittit.	Priscian gives obscure definitions without exposition and in fact leaves out the functional explanations of the various parts of speech and their respective attributes.

The call for clearer definitions is just what one would expect, since Priscian's definitions of his terms are not very rigorous, and additional confusion had resulted from eleventh-century mixing of logical and grammatical terminology (for examples see Kneale & Kneale 1962:199–200 and Hunt 1943:216). The explicit quest for *causae inventionis* was, however, a new development first attested in eleventh-century sources (Hunt

1943:18–19). The idea behind it was that language had been invented in prehistoric times by human beings acting consciously as they assigned (*imposuerunt*) words to signify particular concepts and as they invented (*invenerunt*) linguistic structure. Everything in language was put there to serve a specific function, and the *causa inventionis* of a word or part of speech or grammatical category therefore amounts to an explanation of the communicative function it serves. To give some examples:

Illud quoque sciendum est, quod communis causa inventionis omnium dictionum est ut haberet homo quo modo propriam voluntatem alteri manifestaret. (Petrus Helias, cited by Fredborg 1973:13)

Note also that the functional explanation common to all the parts of speech is this: that a man might have a way to make his will known to another.

Causa inventionis haec est: in omni perfecta oratione dicitur aliquid et de aliquo. Fuit igitur repertum nomen ad discernendum de quo fieret sermo, verbum vero ad discernendum quid dicitur de eo. (Ibid.)

The functional explanation [of the noun and the verb] is this: in every complete sentence something is said, and it is said about something. The noun was therefore introduced to show what the statement was about, and the verb, to indicate what was said about it.

Hic tractat [Priscianus] de cognomine ostendendo quid sit, sed non propriam causam inventionis nec significationem nec nominationem illius dicit. Nos tamen causam inventionis dicamus quae talis est. Cum diversi ab una honesta persona principium generationis haberent ut se de eius familia notarent, nomen illius nomini suo adiungebant et dicebatur cognomen. (William of Conches, comm. on Priscian II.24, first edition [c. 1125], quoted by Fredborg 1973:14)

Here Priscian treats the surname, showing what it is, but he does not say why it was invented, nor what it means, nor what it refers to. But we shall say why it was invented, which is as follows: when various people were descended from one well-known person with the result that they identified themselves as being from his family, they added his name to theirs and it was called a surname.

As the initial confusion about the proper roles of logic and grammar was cleared up, the line between the two fields was drawn in such a way as to place semantics within the province of logic, not grammar. (Priscian, the grammarian par excellence, had after all ignored semantics almost totally, while Aristotle, the logician, had treated it at some length.) The *Dialectica* of Abelard, which de Rijk (1970: xxiii) dates circa 1140, gives a perceptive treatment of the relation between logic and grammar as seen by one philosopher in the middle of the twelfth century. Abelard's treatment of the parts of speech follows Aristotle (*De interpretatione* I–IV), who says that every proposition has two components, the noun and the verb, each of which is an arbitrary linguistic sign no part of which has meaning by itself; the difference between them is that the verb has an extra meaning indicating time (προσσημαίνει χρόνον, *consignificat tempus*), which the noun lacks.

Abelard reconciles Aristotle's doctrine with Priscian's as follows. Conjunctions and prepositions do not have complete meanings by them-selves and are therefore, by Aristotle's criteria, neither nouns nor verbs (*Dialectica*, pp. 118–20); the consideration of them is left to the gram-marian (p. 121). Aristotle's verb obviously comprises Priscian's verb and participle, both of which carry indications of tense. The tenseless linguistic sign, Aristotle's noun, comprises Priscian's noun, pronoun, adverb, and interjection – except that some interjections, such as *ah*, are not arbitrary signs and therefore fall outside the Aristotelian schema (p. 121).[8]

Abelard assumes implicitly that grammar and logic are separate and that it is legitimate for them to deal with the same linguistic phenomena in different ways. Such an assumption is made explicit, both in word and in deed, by the early thirteenth-century *Dialectica Monacensis* (edited by de Rijk, 1967b: 459–638).[9] The author explains that the logician posits only two parts of speech, as opposed to the grammarian's eight, because logic is concerned with relations between whole propositions and does not need to analyze them beyond the division into subject and predicate (pp. 465–6).[10]

The same author's treatment of syntactic ambiguity (*amphibologia*, pp. 565–7) provides striking evidence of the separation of logic from grammar. Taking his cue from Aristotle (*Sophistici elenchi* IV), he discusses a number of ambiguities that involve multiple structural analyses, such as *vidi agnum comedere lupum* ('I saw a wolf eat a lamb' or 'I saw a lamb eat a wolf'), or multiple interpretations of a single structure (*liber Aristotelis*, either 'the book that Aristotle possesses' or 'the book that Aristotle wrote'). One might expect that investigations of this type would be on the forefront of syntactic research, but such is not the case; although the author of the *Dialectica Monacensis* uses such grammatical terminology as he finds convenient, he makes no attempt to contribute to grammatical theory, and his syntactic analysis is actually less sophisticated than that of his predecessor Petrus Helias. The same is true of the various treatises on fallacies edited by de Rijk (1962), whose authors generally turn to paraphrase when rudimentary syntactic analysis fails them, rather than trying to sharpen the tools of syntactic description.

The relation between words and the real-world objects they refer to was likewise a concern of logic, not grammar. Late twelfth-century logicians adopted the term *suppositio* (which means 'presupposition', 'basis', or 'substitution') as their general term for reference; since the time of Priscian, *suppositum* had meant 'presupposed entity', 'topic', or 'referent' in a less rigorously defined sense.[11] In the early thirteenth century Petrus Hispanus and William of Sherwood distinguished many kinds of *suppositio*, ranging from the *suppositio materialis* of a word that is mentioned rather than used (*homo* in *homo est disyllabum*) and the *suppositio simplex* of a word that stands for the concept that constitutes its meaning (*homo est species*) to the more ordinary *suppositio personalis determinata* of a word that refers to one or more members of the class it signifies (*homo currit*, 'a man is running'). The theory of *suppositio* was given less emphasis by the Modistae (Pinborg 1979) and taken up again in the fourteenth century.

The introduction of a clear conceptual distinction between logic (including semantics) and grammar did not mean that anyone tried to do grammatical research without reference to meaning. Quite the contrary: as far as I can determine there was no serious proponent of grammar-without-meaning in the West until Bloomfield (1933). In the Middle Ages, as in traditional grammar generally, it was assumed that communicative function provided the key to understanding the structure of language, and although the study of meaning *per se* was excluded from grammar, grammarians looked to semantic properties to provide criteria for defining the parts of speech, identifying morphological categories, and classifying grammatical relations.

2.3 *Regimen*

The first great medieval contribution to the study of syntax was the development of the concept of government (*regimen*). The origins of *regimen*-theory are obscure; Thurot (1868:82) notes that by the eighth century *regere* was beginning to replace Priscian's term *exigere* in statements that one word requires the presence of, or requires a particular form of, another, and by the early eleventh century there were at least three competing theories of *regimen*.[12]

The doctrine expressed in the didactic grammars of Hugh of St Victor (well before 1141), Alexander de Villa Dei (1199?), and Eberhardus Bethuniensis (1212?)[13] is simple: *regere* means 'require a noun to be in a particular case.'[14] For example, most verbs govern (*regunt*) a nominative subject and an accusative object. Nouns can govern the genitive (*filius Herculis*), the dative (*similis tibi*),[15] and occasionally the accusative (*albus faciem*). The relationship between an adjective and the substantive that it modifies (as in *homo albus*) is not *regimen* because what is required is not some one specific case, but agreement in case whatever the case may be. Further, a case form that is inserted adverbially, such as the ablative absolute, is not subject to any requirement exerted by any other sentence element and is therefore said to be cut off from government (*absolutus a regimine*). (For more on the ablative absolute see section 5.2 below.)

Moreover, in what was to become a standard practice, Hugh of St Victor gave elaborate lists of the basis of each kind of *regimen* in the meaning of the sentence. He says for instance that nouns can govern the genitive by virtue of pre-eminence (*dux militum*), subordination (*servus Domini*), equal status (*socius discipuli*), family relation (*frater Romuli*), other kinds of relationship (*magister puerorum*), possession (*ager agricolae*), and several other things (*De grammatica*, pp. 108–9).[16] The *regimen* of the verb is explained more simply, following Priscianic authority: the verb governs the nominative 'by nature' or 'intransitively' (*intransitione*), and the accusative 'transitively' (cf. Priscian, *Institutiones* XVIII.10).

Among the more theoretically oriented grammarians there were attempts to develop the concept of *regimen* into something more general. A number of twelfth-century Priscian commentaries studied by Kneepkens (1978) present theories of *regimen* in connection with the following passage:

Et sciendum quod has quidem constructiones, quae per nominativum absolvuntur, Stoici ἀζιώματα vel συμβάματα, id est dignitates vel congruitates, vocabant – ut 'ego Priscianus	Note that these constructions, which are made complete by nominatives, were called by the Stoics ἀξιώματα or συμβάματα, i.e., 'worthinesses' or 'compatibilities' – for example 'I,

scribo', 'Apollonius ambulat', 'Plato philosophatur' – illas vero, quibus transitiones ab alia ad aliam fiunt personam, in quibus necesse est cum nominativo etiam obliquum aliquem casum proferri, παρασυμβάματα dicebant, hoc est minus quam congruitates, ut 'Cicero servat patriam'; quando vero ex duobus obliquis constructio fit, ἀσύμβαμα, id est incongruitatem, dicebant, ut 'placet mihi venire ad te', sive nominibus ipsis tamen seu verbis hoc exigentibus. (Priscian, *Institutiones* XVIII.4–5)

Priscian, write', 'Apollonius walks around', and 'Plato philosophizes'. The ones in which the action proceeds from one person to another, and in which it is necessary to use an oblique case form as well as the nominative, were called παρασυμβάματα 'less than compatibilities', such as 'Cicero protects the nation'. When a construction is formed from two obliques [and no nominative] they called it an ἀσύμβαμα or 'incompatibility', for example '(it) pleases me to come to you', whether it is the nouns themselves or the [complement] verbs that exert this requirement.

Priscian's account of Stoic syntactic theory is muddled here.[17] In normal Stoic usage an ἀξίωμα is a complete proposition, composed of subject and predicate. A σύμβαμα is a predicate that takes a nominative subject, e.g. περιπατεῖ, 'walks around', while a παρασύμβαμα is an impersonal predicate that takes a noun in a case other than the nominative, for example μεταμέλει, which governs the dative in the sentence Σωκράτει μεταμέλει, 'Socrates is sorry'. The term ἐλάττον ἢ σύμβαμα, 'less than a σύμβαμα', refers to a predicate that requires an object as well as a subject and is obviously not at all the same thing as a παρασύμβαμα, with which Priscian confuses it. To give some examples, φιλεῖ, 'loves', is ἐλάττον ἢ σύμβαμα, Δίωνα φιλεῖ, 'loves Dion', is a σύμβαμα, and Πλάτων Δίωνα φιλεῖ, 'Plato loves Dion', is an ἀξίωμα. To round out the system, a verb that requires two obliques is called ἐλάττον ἢ παρασύμβαμα (and not, as Priscian says, ἀσύμβαμα). The standard definitions of παρασύμβαμα and ἐλάττον ἢ παρασύμβαμα are given by Apollonius (*On Syntax* III.187), whom Priscian contradicts; a fuller account of the system is given by Porphyry, quoted by Ammonius (*Stoicorum veterum fragmenta* II.184).

In any event, the small fragments of Stoic syntactic theory that Priscian happened to pass along had no substantial influence on medieval grammar except, perhaps, as a tantalizing indication that a complete theory of syntax could be built around the concept of government.[18] For the materials out of which to construct such a theory the medievals turned to contemporary philosophy.

The earliest known extension of *regimen*-theory beyond mere morphological determination is that presented in the Priscian commentary of one Magister Guido, dating from around 1100 or 1110, before the disentanglement of logic and grammar (Kneepkens 1978). Guido identifies *regimen* with the semantic relationship of *determinatio* (removal of vagueness or ambiguity) defined in Boethius' *De divisione*. He explains:

Sicut enim aliquis errans in via eget alicuius regimine ut ad viam redeat et per viam certus eat, sic dictiones pleraeque in constructione positae, per aliquam incertitudinem quam habent circa suam significationem, egent aliarum coniunctione dictionum a quibus regantur, id est ab illa incertitudine quam habent removeantur et certum quid significare monstrentur. (Kneepkens 1978:128)

Just as someone who gets lost on a journey needs the guidance of someone else in order to return to the right road and proceed with certainty, in the same way many words placed in syntactic structure, because of some inherent uncertainty about their meaning, require the addition of other words to govern them, i.e, to free them from the uncertainty that they bear and show that they mean something specific.

Guido claims that in a sentence like *Socrates currit*, 'Socrates runs', *Socrates* is in some sense vague and indefinite without the verb *currit*, which governs and 'determines' it.

The obvious question arises: does *currit* determine *Socrates* or does *Socrates* determine *currit*? One could argue that there is *determinatio* running in both directions: *Socrates* is clear with regard to who is being talked about, but unclear with regard to what is being said about him, while *currit* is clear as to what is being said but not who it is being said about, so that each of the two words makes the other less vague. Guido acknowledges this and contents himself with a rather unconvincing statement that there is more *determinatio* running from *currit* to *Socrates* (in the same direction as the *regimen*) than vice versa.

The reason Guido did not say that the *regimen* in *Socrates currit* goes in both directions, like the *determinatio*, is that, like all the early *regimen*-theorists, he knew in advance how the *regimen* had to come out; he took *regit* as meaning the same as Priscian's *exigit, construitur cum,* and *refertur ad* (Kneepkens 1978:124), even though these terms did not have the technical status for Priscian that *regit* had for the medievals. Based on his interpretation of Priscian, Guido assumed that the verb governed the subject and object, the noun governed various oblique cases, the preposition governed its object, and so forth; the challenge was to find a theoretically well-defined relation that followed this pattern.

Determinatio turned out to be such an unreliable criterion that a number of grammarians had no difficulty claiming that the correspondence between *determinatio* and *regimen* was exactly the opposite of what Guido had said – i.e., that the governed word *determinat* the governing one, rather than vice versa. Such a view is represented in the logical writings of Abelard (Kneepkens 1978:128–9).

Petrus Helias examines such a theory and rejects it.[19] He argues of course that *determinatio* is no help in determining whether the verb governs the subject or vice versa. Further, he points out that if *determinatio* and *regimen* run in opposite directions, then since the preposition *determinat* its object, the object must govern the preposition, which is absurd ('quod caret ratione,' *Summa* on *Priscianus minor,* p. 154). He proposes a completely different theory, in which the governing element requires the governed element 'for the completeness of the construction' – to be more precise, the governed element identifies the real-world referent to which the meaning of the governing element applies.

Propter haec ergo et alia plura nolo dicere quod regere dictionem sit eam adiungere sibi in constructione ad determinationem suae significationis, sed ut brevius et verius dicam, dictionem regere dictionem nihil aliud est quam trahere secum eam in constructione ad constructionis perfectionem, non autem dico ad significationis determinationem. (p. 154)

For these and many other reasons, therefore, I do not wish to say that to govern a word is to have it adjoined in syntactic structure to make the governing word's meaning more specific, but, to put it more succinctly and more accurately, for a word to govern another is nothing other than for it to bring it into construction with itself in order to make the construction complete – I do not say in order to make its meaning specific.

Cum enim dico 'Socrates' non intellego statim rem ut de ea dicitur res verbi, sicut cum dico 'legit' designo rem ut dicitur de re nominis. Non ergo nominativus trahit verbum in constructionem, sed verbum nominativum ad perfectionem constructionis. Idcirco verbum regit nominativum casum, nominativus vero non regit verbum.

For when I say 'Socrates' I do not immediately think of its referent [i.e., Socrates himself] as being something of which the meaning of a verb is predicated, in the way that when I say 'reads' I refer to reading as something predicated of the referent of a noun. The nominative therefore does not bring the verb into the construction; the verb brings in the nominative in order to make the construction complete. So the verb governs the nominative, not vice versa.

Si opponatur quia secundum hoc praepositio non regit obliquum casum quia non trahit obliquum in constructionem, immo magis obliquus trahit praepositionem, dico hoc esse falsum, quia praepositio trahit obliquum in constructione⟨m⟩. Cum enim dico 'averto faciem meam ab illo', ibi 'averto' significat separationem, quae separatio etiam significatur per praepositionem quia praepositio significat separationem, sed non determinat cuius rei. Idcirco necessario trahit secum obliquum per quem separatio illa certificetur. Unde praepositio obliquum casum habet regere. (p. 155)

If someone objects that by this criterion the preposition does not govern the oblique case form because it does not bring the oblique into the construction, but rather the oblique brings the preposition into the construction, I say that this is false; the preposition does bring the oblique into the construction. For when I say 'I turn my face away from him', the 'I turn away' signifies separation, and the preposition also signifies separation but does not specify from what. Therefore it necessarily brings with it an oblique case form by means of which the separation can be made definite. Hence the preposition has to govern the oblique case.

He goes on to explain that the verb governs the object as well as the subject because a transitive verb such as *legit*, 'reads', signifies an action proceeding from one real-world referent to another – a Priscianic *transitio per-sonarum* – and is therefore incomplete unless both referents are specified, as in *Socrates legit Vergilium*.[20] In the case of a noun substantive governing an oblique, as in *pater filii*, it would appear that the governing element, being a substantive, already has a real-world referent and does not need a governed element to provide one, but Petrus claims that in such cases the governing noun signifies a relationship (*ex vi relativa*) rather than an entity in itself: in response to *pater* the hearer awaits an indication of whose father it is ('auditor semper expectat cuius pater,' p. 156).

The scheme that Petrus Helias outlines in his chapter on *regimen* is the following, indicating *regimen* with arrows pointing from governing element to governed:

verb + nominative	*Socrates ← legit*
verb + oblique	*legit → Vergilium*
noun + oblique	*pater → filii*
	similis → illi
adverb + oblique	*similiter → illi*
preposition + oblique	*ab → illo*

This is of course only a sampling, but by putting it together with Petrus' more Priscianic statements, throughout the commentary, about what *exigit* or *construitur cum* what, the system can easily be extended to cover a wide range of Latin constructions. The 'noun + oblique' category, for instance, applies to substantives and adjectives governing any oblique case, as in *vir magna virtute* (p. 133), *fortior illo* (p. 134), *albus dentem* (p. 138), and so forth. One of his more interesting analyses is that in a passive with an expressed agent, such as *doceor a te*, the agent *te* is governed both by the verb and by the preposition.

Note that the governed element is always a noun or pronoun (or a participle functioning as a noun). In Petrus' theory, this is so because only nouns and pronouns refer to things (as opposed to actions or relations) in the real world. According to the morphological criterion used by the didactic grammarians, the governed element has to be a noun or pronoun because to govern is to require a specific case, and only nouns and pronouns are inflected for case.

Petrus Helias' account of *regimen* was transmitted faithfully to the Modistae of the next century, but it was by no means the last word on the subject. The theory that *regimen* equals *determinatio* (but runs in the opposite direction) was still being taught by Ralph of Beauvais some decades later, and in the theoretical work of the late twelfth-century grammarian Robert Blund the didactic grammarians' morphological criterion had won out (Kneepkens 1978).

2.4 Grammar as theoretical science

Between the middle of the twelfth century and the middle of the thirteenth, grammarians' conception of what they were doing underwent a radical change. Even for a philosophical grammarian as sophisticated as William of Conches, grammar was an *ars* whose primary aim was to teach people to write better Latin;[21] but within a century afterward, grammar had been reclassified as a theoretical science on a level with physics and mathematics.

The motivation for this change came ultimately from Aristotle's *Posterior Analytics* and Alfarabi's *Liber de scientiis*, both of which became available in northern Europe in the mid 1100s. The rediscovery of the *Posterior Analytics* and the remainder of Aristotle's logical works led to a methodological revolution in which Aristotle's criteria for scientific knowledge were applied to all fields of study. Tredennick (1938:7) summarizes these criteria as follows:

> Scientific knowledge is concerned only with necessary facts; these can only be known as necessary if they are proved as such; therefore the premises from which they are proved must be necessary. They must also be scientific; and this implies certain relations between predicate and subject. (1) The predicate must be true of *all* of the subject. (2) The predicate must be essential to the subject, or the subject to the predicate. (3) The predicate must be true of the subject considered strictly as itself, not as a member of a higher class.[22]

The object of scientific knowledge is that which could not be otherwise (ἀδύνατον ἄλλως ἔχειν, *quod non potest aliter se habere*), and the goal of scientific inquiry is to find the necessary first principles from which it can be deduced. This means that physics, for instance, is concerned with principles that apply to all possible physical changes (or to exhaustive subclassifications of them), not just to those changes that happen actually to have occurred. Medieval grammarians reasoned that, by the same criteria, the scientific study of language would have to state principles applicable to all possible languages, not just the one under study.

A hint as to how this might be done came from Alfarabi, who divided the knowledge of language into word-knowledge, comprising arbitrary details, and rule-knowledge, comprising generalizations ('orationes universales,' *Liber de scientiis*, p. 121).[23] His mid-twelfth-century translator and expositor Dominicus Gundissalinus went further: he identified rule-knowledge with syntax ('scientia ordinandi singulas dictiones in oratione ad significandum conceptiones animae') and stated that, unlike vocabulary, rule-knowledge was practically the same for all peoples ('paene eadem apud omnes secundum similitudinem regularum,' *De divisione philosophiae*, pp. 45–6).

In the *Priscianus minor* commentary of one Magister Jordanus (c. 1230/ 50), Alfarabi's (or rather his translators') term *scientia linguae* had been replaced by *scientia sermocinalis* – the term used also in Robert Kilwardby's *De ortu scientiarum* and practically all subsequent works – and by the middle of the thirteenth century a number of philosophers had come to the conclusion that grammar was a science in the Aristotelian sense and that the universals it sought had something to do with syntax and semantics. To quote Roger Bacon:

Grammatica una et eadem est secundum substantiam in omnibus linguis, licet accidentaliter varietur. (*Greek Grammar*, p. 27)	With regard to its substance, grammar is one and the same in all languages, though it may be subject to inessential variation.

Magister Jordanus is more specific:

Licet voces inquantum voces non sint eaedem apud omnes, tamen secundum modum ordinandi et secundum intellectum quem constituunt sunt eaedem apud omnes. (*Notulae*, p. 5)	Though words in and of themselves may not be the same for all people, nonetheless they are the same for all people with regard to the way they are put together and the meaning they convey.

It was then only a short step from *scientia* to *scientia speculativa*. Aristotle had classified knowledge as practical or theoretical (πρακτική/θεωρητική, *practica/speculativa*) depending on whether its aim was action or simply truth for its own sake (*Metaphysics* II.1.5, 993 b 21–2), and this distinction naturally figured in medieval classifications of the sciences (especially those influenced by the *Metaphysics* of Algazel, in which *practica/speculativa* is treated as the highest-order distinction, dividing all the sciences into two groups). The last major classification in which grammar is explicitly *practica* is that of Robert Kilwardby (c. 1250. *De ortu scientiarum*, chs. 46, 47);

grammar is *speculativa* for Pseudo-Kilwardby (pp. 30–2), Vincent of Beauvais (fl. 1244–64, *Speculum doctrinale* I.18), and all the Modistae (at least until modistic grammar began dying out; but see Pinborg 1967:106).

The primary goal of *grammatica speculativa*, like that of modern linguistic theory, was to find universals of language, but the basically Aristotelian methodology of the medievals made the nature of their quest rather different from its modern counterpart. According to the *Posterior Analytics*, a scientific statement has to be not merely true, but *necessarily* true, of all the members of the class it describes. From the medieval grammarian's point of view, then, the superficial comparison of a large number of languages would be of little use to the science of grammar; many shared properties would of course emerge, but there would be no way to tell which of these were genuine universals, essential to language, and which were spurious, accidental shared properties that could easily have been otherwise. In any case, the first principles sought by speculative grammar were so abstract that one could hardly expect to discover them without extensive, penetrating analysis. The obvious first order of business was therefore to discover as much as possible about how the properties of one well-known, intensively studied language follow from the essence of language itself. For this reason, then, even though it had long been recognized that philosophical grammar could be applied to Greek and Hebrew and even French (Fredborg 1980), and although references to Greek turned up occasionally in modistic grammar (see section 3.2 below), the Modistae confined the main thrust of their research program to Latin.

3 *Modistic grammar*

The Modistae were a group of grammarians and logicians,[1] active principally at Paris during the second half of the thirteenth century, who held that in addition to having a pronunciation and a meaning, every word has a set of properties called *modi significandi* (modes of signifying) that determine how the particular meaning is encoded into the language. For example, the verb *currere*, 'to run', and the noun *cursus*, 'a run', signify the same thing – the act of running; the difference between them is that they signify it in different ways (under different modes). *Currere* signifies running conceived of as an act or change in progress (*per modum fluxus et fieri*); *cursus* signifies it as an enduring entity (*per modum habitus et permanentiae*). Modes of signifying account not only for the differences between the various parts of speech, but also for all the other properties of a word that reside neither in its meaning (in the strict sense) nor in its pronunciation – including such things as gender, number, case, and form (simple or complex).

3.1 The Modistae

Only a small part of the vast literature of medieval grammar has been printed or even read through in modern times. Nonetheless, by studying many unedited manuscripts as well as all available printed editions, Pinborg (1967) has been able to trace the main outlines of the development of modistic grammar, and subsequent research has contributed many details to the picture. In this section I shall summarize and update Pinborg's results, with emphasis on the medieval grammarians whose works constitute the data for the present study.

Modism arose out of speculative grammar in the mid 1200s as the concept of *modus significandi* assumed a more and more prominent role in the analysis of language. There was, of course, an initial 'pre-modistic' period, lasting until about 1260, during which the concept of *modus signi-*

ficandi was utilized to define the parts of speech but had not yet been applied to syntax in more than a superficial way.[2] Important pre-modistic authors include Magister Jordanus (c. 1230/50); Roger Bacon (*Summa grammatica*, c. 1240); Johannes le Rus, Robert Kilwardby, and Pseudo-Kilwardby (all c. 1250); and Goswin of Marbais and Simon Dacus Domifex[3] (both c. 1260). Further, treatises that are pre-modistic or semi-modistic in content were written at much later dates by authors who did not assimilate modism in its entirety, such as Thomas de Hancya (1313).

The first generation of Modistae proper begins with Martin of Dacia (Denmark), whose *Modi significandi* became a standard textbook almost immediately.[4] Written in a particularly clear expository style, it represented the first thorough attempt to make modes of signifying the basis of all grammatical analysis, including syntax, and it established the standard format for the *tractatus de modis significandi*: a brief metatheoretical preamble followed by an enumeration of the modes of signifying of the various parts of speech (*Etymologia*) and a discussion of syntax (*Diasynthetica* or *Diasyntactica*, often misspelled). Particularly on matters of metatheory and syntax, Martin is consciously innovative to a degree unusual in the Middle Ages; he often says things like 'Communiter dicitur ... Ego autem dico ...'.

Other important treatises from the first generation include the *Quaestiones super Priscianum maiorem* (*Modi significandi*) of Boethius Dacus (c. 1270), which are extremely thorough and well thought out, though the syntactic section has unfortunately been lost, and the thorough but unfinished *Summa grammaticae* of Johannes Dacus (1280), which in the equivalent of 511 printed pages gets no further than the *etymologia* of the noun. The unedited *Doctrinale* commentary of Petrus Croccus (c. 1275) is a particularly useful source of information about early modistic syntactic theory.

Michael of Marbais, whose works are unfortunately also still unedited, represents the latter years of the first generation of Modistae; besides his *Modi significandi singularum partium orationis* (c. 1285, quoted extensively by Thurot 1868), we now have his *Priscianus minor* commentary, at least if Pinborg's tentative identification is correct.[5] The doctrines represented in the *Quaestiones Alberti de modis significandi* of Pseudo-Albertus Magnus belong to the same period, though Pinborg has suggested that the treatise itself may be a later compilation.[6]

The second generation of Modistae comprises the period of culmination from about 1285 until the onslaught of nominalist attacks in the early

1300s. The first sign that a stage of maturity has been reached is the appearance of commentaries on the works of earlier Modistae, especially Martin of Dacia. Pinborg (1967:314–15) lists twelve commentaries on Martin's *Modi significandi*; all of them are still unedited, and the only ones I have been able to consult are the one by Albertus Swebelinus (c. 1290/1300) and the 'Turpe est ignorare', which Pinborg has tentatively attributed to Simon Dacus Modista (c. 1285/90). From Simon we have also a set of questions on the last book of Priscian (*Quaestiones super secundum minoris voluminis Prisciani*), edited by Alfred Otto (1963).

Modistic grammar reached the height of its development during the first two decades of the fourteenth century at Paris among a group of moderate Aristotelian philosophers centered around Radulphus Brito, who himself was a thinker of wide-ranging interests and whose importance to general medieval philosophy has probably been underestimated. In addition to the thorough *Quaestiones super Priscianum minorem* of Radulphus, we have a *Summa modorum significandi* and several *Sophismata* (brief discussions of apparent paradoxes or difficult points) by Siger de Courtrai and, more importantly, the *Novi modi significandi* (*Grammatica speculativa*) of Thomas of Erfurt, which successfully replaced Martin of Dacia's work as the standard handbook of modistic grammar.[7] Though the two expound virtually the same theory, there is a sharp contrast between Radulphus, the theoretician who delights in discovering difficulties and laying them bare, and Thomas, the pedagogue whose goal is to present a consistent position with the difficulties smoothed over. (Siger is a theoretician like Radulphus, but less prolific.) Two other treatises from the same period are those referred to by Enders and Pinborg (1980), on the basis of the present locations of the manuscripts, as Anonymus Norimbergensis and Anonymus Cracoviensis; both are sets of questions on *Priscianus minor*.

The development of modistic theory ground to a halt in the early decades of the fourteenth century as the doctrine of modes of signifying proved incompatible with the nominalist philosophy that was then gaining popularity. The theory itself, however, continued to be taught, in frozen form, for some time. There were brief attempts to apply modistic theory to the teaching of elementary Latin grammar to schoolboys; among those who sought to do so were Thomas of Erfurt himself, whose works include an elementary *Fundamentum puerorum*[8] laced with modistic terminology, and Thomas de Hancya, whose non-theoretically-oriented handbook of grammar (dated 1313) includes modistic terminology as well as that of the older didactic tradition. Even apart from its influence on didactic grammar, modism proved quite persistent: in 1322 Johannes Josse composed a modistic grammatical treatise in verse for easy memorization, showing that university courses in modistic grammar were still going strong, and as late as the beginning of the sixteenth century, Johannes Stobnicensis wrote a *Compendiosa descriptio* to explain modism to a young gentleman studying at Cracow.[9]

3.2 Modes of signifying

The concept of *modus significandi* was developed as a simultaneous solution to a number of philosophical problems connected with grammar, among them the following:

(1) Why are the parts of speech what they are? That is, what is there in the essential nature of language that causes words to fall into eight distinct and exhaustive classes – nouns, verbs, participles, pronouns, adverbs, prepositions, conjunctions, interjections, and nothing else?
(2) How does inflectional meaning – for instance, the element of time signified by the tense of the verb – relate to lexical meaning?
(3) What aspects of the structure of language follow necessarily from the structure of cognition and of the real world?
(4) What properties of words enable them to be put together to form syntactic structures?

The Modistae subsumed questions (2), (3), and (4) under (1), ending up with the more basic question: what are the attributes of words, and why are they what they are? After all, a comprehensive theory of the attributes of words (or rather the scientifically interesting, non-arbitrary ones) would at once explicate the classification of the parts of speech, the nature of inflectional meaning, the cognitive basis of linguistic structure (as the origin of some of the attributes of words), and the ability of words to form larger structures.

In what follows I shall keep the four problems distinct and examine them one by one. It should be emphasized that the logical order I have chosen for exposition does not necessarily match the historical order in which the various parts of modistic theory were developed.

The Modistae found Priscian's definitions of the parts of speech philosophically unsatisfying. As illustrated in the samples quoted in section 2.1 above, Priscian's definitions appealed to a variety of apparently unrelated criteria – inflection, syntax, and meaning – often using completely different criteria to identify different parts of speech and thus failing to indicate what universal principle, if any, underlay the structure of the complete set.[10] Yet the Modistae thought it necessary to find such a principle. In their view, the scientific study of language had to begin with the principled identification and classification of its component parts, which were obviously the *partes orationis*. Further, such a classification should refer to the essence of language – its ability to convey meaning – and should exclude such arbitrary, language-specific details as morphology or distribution. This being so, it would seem that the parts of speech ought to be distinguished on the basis of meaning – but this is impossible, since the same meaning can be expressed by different parts of speech (as in *currere* and *cursus*, mentioned above, or Boethius Dacus' more striking set of four: *dolor*, 'pain', *doleo*, 'I feel pain', *dolenter*, 'painfully', and *heu*, 'ouch!' [*Quaestiones* 14, p. 56]).

In earlier speculative grammar there had been attempts to distinguish a *significatio generalis*, shared by all words that belong to the same class, from the *significatio specialis* of each word individually;[11] but modism provided a much more satisfactory way out of the dilemma by endowing words with properties – the modes of signifying – that were at once suitable for distinguishing the parts of speech, and explicitly connected with the significative function of language. In modistic theory, words can differ either in what they signify, or in how they signify it, or both. *Currere* and *cursus* signify the same thing under different modes and are therefore different parts of speech; *currere*, 'run', and *ambulare*, 'walk', being the same part of speech, signify different things under the same mode.

In holding that the parts of speech were identified by modes of signifying, and that modes of signifying were non-arbitrary, the Modistae came near to committing themselves to the belief that the parts of speech had to be the same in all languages; yet they were aware that Greek had a definite article, which Latin lacked. They commonly dealt with this fact by saying, erroneously, that Greek nouns are indeclinable and that the article serves the same function as the Latin case ending:[12]

Et cum dicitur, 'Graeci habent aliquam partem orationis quam non habemus, scilicet articulum,' dico quod articulus non est principaliter pars orationis, sed accidentaliter est inventa apud Graecos scilicet ad distinctionem

In response to the objection that the Greeks have a part of speech that we lack, namely the article, I say that the article is not a part of speech in the most basic sense, but happens to have been invented by the Greeks in order to distinguish

casuum et generum, quia voces in Graeco sunt indistinctae in casibus et generibus, sicut 'antropos' habetur in quolibet casu. Ideo aliqui articuli sunt inventi ad distinguendum casus. (Radulphus Brito, *Quaestiones* I.1, pp. 91–2)

cases and genders. Greek words are not marked for case and gender, so that for example the form *antropos* is retained in all the cases [*sic*]. Therefore articles were invented to mark the cases.

The Greek article was the only non-Latin grammatical phenomenon routinely mentioned in modistic treatises, since the Modistae were much more concerned with achieving a perceptive analysis of one language than with language comparison. Nonetheless, broader questions of the significance of universal grammar did arise. It seemed superficially absurd to say that grammar was the same in all languages, since anyone not understanding the very special and abstract meaning of 'grammar' in the context of this claim would be likely to think that the Modistae were denying the obvious. Boethius Dacus dealt with this objection as follows:

Cum dicis, si omnia idiomata sint una grammatica, tunc qui sciret eam in uno, sciret eam in alio idiomate, concedo consequentiam ... quantum ad omnia ea quae sunt essentialia grammaticae. Quod autem sciens grammaticam in uno idiomate non loquitur in alio idiomate nec intelligit hominem loquentem in alio, causa est diversitas vocum et figuratio diversa earundem, quae accidentalis est grammaticae, sicut dictum est. (pp. 13–14)

When you say that if all languages had the same grammar, then whoever knew the grammar of one language would know the grammar of any other language also, I agree that this follows ... with regard to everything that is essential to grammar. But as for the fact that a person who knows the grammar of one language does not speak another language or understand a person speaking another language, the reason is the diversity of word-forms and the different ways of forming them, which is not an essential part of grammar, as already stated.

The Modistae were interested only in what they considered the essence of grammar, not the language-specific and arbitrary details.

The question of how inflectional meaning relates to lexical meaning was first raised, at least implicitly, by Aristotle, who pointed out that one of the most prominent differences between the verb and the noun is that the verb is marked for tense – that is, in addition to its lexical meaning, the verb always carries an extra indication of time (προσσημαίνει χρόνον, *consignificat tempus*).[13] Commenting on Aristotle's text, the philosopher Boethius noted further that verb tense is not at all like the lexical indication of time in words like 'today' or 'tomorrow' ('aliud est enim significare tempus, aliud consignificare'), but he said nothing about the reason for the difference except that the verb signifies time *cum aliquo proprio modo*, 'with some mode of its own.'[14]

Roughly, the problem was that of explaining why part of the meaning of a sentence such as 'Socrates walked' or 'Socrates will walk' is hidden in the inflection of the verb. The sharp distinction between meaning, which is essential to the communicative function of language, and inflection, which is accidental, appears to be breaking down; the meaning of a tensed sentence is not purely a function of the lexical items of which it is composed plus the structure into which they are arranged.

The modistic solution was to bridge the gap between inflection and meaning by treating *all* inflectional categories – including tense – as *modi significandi*, and to claim that they all relate to meaning in the same way, though the relation is more obvious in some instances than in others. According to Martin of Dacia (pp. 58–60), the tense of the verb is not in itself part of the meaning; it is a *modus significandi* that makes it possible for the verb to indicate (*consignificare*) a particular property of the thing signified, namely the time at which the action takes place. In fully developed modistic theory, all modes of signifying are held to be, in one way or another, representations of the properties of real-world objects; that is, all *modi significandi* are *rationes consignificandi*. Tense 'consignifies' time; the singular and plural in grammar are representations of singularity and plurality of real objects; and the noun–verb distinction mirrors[15] the distinction between substance and process in the real world.

At this point a difficulty arises. If all inflectional categories are modes of signifying, how can modes of signifying serve as an essential, universal basis for defining the parts of speech? After all, some inflectional categories – verb tense among them – are neither essential nor universal. It is easy to imagine a language that lacks verb tense but, by using adverbs or some other mechanism to express time, achieves the same expressive power as Latin or Greek; this proves that tense is not an essential attribute of the verb.[16] The definition of the verb therefore cannot mention tense.

What emerges is the distinction between essential and accidental modes of signifying. To quote Thomas of Erfurt:

Modus significandi essentialis est per quem pars orationis habet simpliciter esse, vel secundum genus vel secundum speciem. Modus significandi accidentalis est qui advenit parti post eius esse completum, non dans esse simpliciter parti, nec secundum genus nec secundum speciem. (*Grammatica speculativa*, p. 148).

An essential mode of signifying is that by virtue of which a part of speech is what it is, with regard to either class (e.g., 'noun') or subclass (e.g., 'proper noun'). An accidental mode of signifying is what is added to a part of speech after it has all its essential features; the accidental mode does not, in itself, make the part of speech what it is, either with regard to class or with regard to subclass.

The essential modes of signifying distinguish the various parts of speech, as well as making subordinate distinctions such as those between proper and common nouns, between substantives and adjectives, between cardinal and ordinal numerals, and the like. Accidental modes comprise such things as gender, number, case, person, voice, mood, tense, and derivational relationships between words.

Some of the accidental modes mirror properties, not of the thing signified by the word to which they belong, but of the thing signified by some other word in the sentence. For instance, the number of the verb represents, not the singularity or plurality of the action that the verb signifies, but the singularity or plurality of the subject. This led the Modistae to divide the accidental modes into two classes, *absoluti* and *respectivi*:

Mod⟨or⟩um significandi accidentalium quidam sunt absoluti, quidam respectivi. Modi significandi absoluti sunt qui solum referuntur ad rei proprietatem et non ad modum significandi alterius constructibilis, sicut est figura et tempus in verbo ... Modi significandi respectivi sunt qui non solum referuntur ad rei pro-

Some accidental modes of signifying are absolute; others are respective (relative). The absolute modes of signifying are those that are related solely to a property of the thing signified and not to a mode of signifying on the part of another word; examples are the morphological type and tense of the verb ... The respective modes

prietates, sed etiam and modos significandi in alio constructibili. (Radulphus Brito, I.17, pp. 144–5)

of signifying are those that refer not merely to the properties of the thing signified, but also to modes of signifying on the part of another word.

(A *constructibile* is a word considered as a syntactic unit; see Chapter 4.)

That is, a respective mode is one that a word picks up from another word through grammatical agreement processes; an absolute mode is one that it possesses on its own. Practically all the Modistae, both early and late, make this distinction; Martin of Dacia stands out by never mentioning it. (Siger de Courtrai interprets the respective – absolute distinction a bit differently, as dividing modes that are relevant to syntax from those that are not, and applies it to essential as well as accidental modes [*sophisma* 'Amo est verbum', p. 43]; so does the author of two marginal annotations to the Radulphus Brito passage just quoted.)[17]

To survey the complete modistic theory of the relation of language to the real world would take us far afield from the present study; moreover, it has already been studied in depth by modern scholars.[18] However, it is both appropriate and necessary to give an overview. The theory exists in two versions, differing as to whether they distinguish *modi activi* and *passivi*; the earlier version, which lacks the distinction, is that of Boethius Dacus, Martin of Dacia, and Johannes Dacus, while the later version, making the distinction, is that used by Michael of Marbais, Pseudo-Albertus, and virtually all later writers.

The early version of the theory, as set forth by Martin of Dacia (pp. 6–9), holds that every real-world object has not only an essence, which makes it what it is, but also a set of *modi essendi*, 'modes of being', various properties that allow it to be conceived of in various ways. Thus, along with its *conceptus* of the thing itself, the intellect has access to *modi intelligendi*, various 'modes of understanding' that derive from the properties of the object that are 'co-understood' (*cointelliguntur*) along with the thing itself. The linguistic sign, in turn, signifies the concept (or rather signifies the thing via the concept) and consignifies the modes of understanding (or consignifies various properties of the thing by way of the *modi intelligendi*); the consignified properties are called *modi significandi*. The whole system, as set out by Martin of Dacia (pp. 6–9), can be diagrammed as shown in Figure 1.[19]

Later Modistae noticed a difficulty. According to this schema, the modes

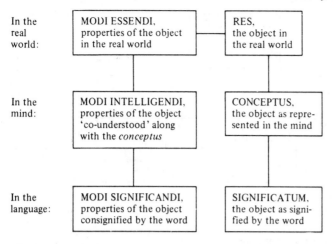

In the real world:	MODI ESSENDI, properties of the object in the real world	RES, the object in the real world
In the mind:	MODI INTELLIGENDI, properties of the object 'co-understood' along with the *conceptus*	CONCEPTUS, the object as represented in the mind
In the language:	MODI SIGNIFICANDI, properties of the object consignified by the word	SIGNIFICATUM, the object as signified by the word

Figure 1. Ontology of the modes of signifying (Martin of Dacia)

of signifying are the real-world properties that are consignified by words. Since grammar is defined as the study of modes of signifying, it should follow that grammar is the study of the consignified properties, such as time, position, plurality, and the like – which is not the case. Grammar is actually the study, not of the properties themselves, but of the mechanisms or means by which the properties are encoded into language. Apparently for this reason, Boethius Dacus adopted a quite different approach. He viewed modes of signifying, not as properties of the real-world object consignified by the word (e.g., time, consignified by verb tense), but as the attributes of the word that make the consignification possible (e.g., verb tense itself); as Pinborg put it, 'Der *modus significandi* ist also nicht ein Inhalt, sondern er hat einen' (1967:82).

Later Modistae combined the two approaches by distinguishing between *modi significandi activi*, 'modes of signifying', which are properties of the word, and *modi significandi passivi*, 'modes of being signified',[20] which are the properties of the real-world object that the word consignifies. Corresponding to these, of course, are modes of understanding and of being understood, and it is the *modi intelligendi passivi* rather than *activi* that correspond to the *modi essendi*, as shown in Figure 2. (Relative to the combined schema, Martin had only *modi passivi*, and Boethius had only *modi activi*.) Most Modistae went on to define grammar as the study of *modi significandi activi*, and all was well.[21]

The speculative grammarians of the Middle Ages, both modistic and

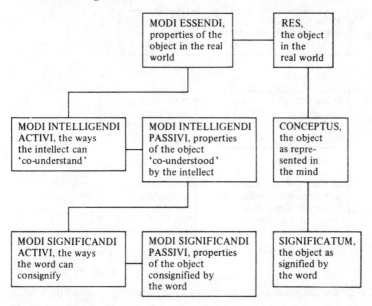

Figure 2. Ontology of the modes of signifying (Thomas of Erfurt)

pre-modistic, held that one of the most important characteristics of language, as against other sign-systems, is that the elements of language can be linked together, so that language expresses not merely concepts, but compound concepts (*conceptus compositi*). Not only can one say 'Socrates' and 'philosopher'; one can also link the two together and form, not just an aggregate that means 'Socrates, philosopher' and leaves it to the hearer to figure out exactly what relation between the two is meant, but rather a sentence, 'Socrates is a philosopher', that makes the relation clear by its structure.

The linking together of linguistic signs is called *constructio*, a term which in Priscian means 'syntax' and which gradually acquires a more technical meaning as modistic grammar develops; I shall translate it by 'construction' and refer to the things that undergo construction, the *constructibilia*, as 'constructibles'. Thomas of Hancya defines construction as follows:

Dicendum quod construere est constructibilia per suos modos significandi sic unire ut possit iunctis exprimi conceptus unus. (Bodleian ms. 643, fol. 231v)

To establish construction is to join constructibles by means of their modes of signifying in such a way that together they can express a single concept.

The Modistae are naturally concerned with finding out what it is that makes construction possible (*quid sit principium constructionis*). Since the properties of words fall into three sets, there are three possibilities: *vox* (pronunciation), *significatum* (meaning), and *modi significandi*. Of these, *vox* can be eliminated immediately, since the pronounced form of the word is completely arbitrary and accidental, while construction is part of the essential nature of language. It is equally obvious that meaning is not the sole basis of syntax, as Johannes le Rus points out:

Dictiones enim habentes eandem significationem exigunt constructiones oppositas sicut 'currere' et 'currens' – eandem habent significationem, non autem eandem constructionem. Quare cum diversificentur, et non per significatum, oportet quod diversificentur penes accidentia. (*Quaestiones* 7, Vatican ms., fol. 92ra)	Words that have the same meaning require different constructions, like the verb *currere* and the participle *currens* – they have the same meaning but not the same construction. For this reason, since they differ, but not in meaning, it follows that they differ in their other characteristics.

That leaves the modes of signifying, which are the most important *principia constructionis*; but there remains also the question of whether meaning is involved at all. Petrus Helias says that it is, citing Priscian's statement that 'every construction ... is to be related to the understanding of the word-form'[22] and claiming that semantically deviant sentences such as 'Socrates has hypothetical shoes with categorical shoelaces' (which mixes object language with metalanguage) contain faulty constructions.[23] Magister Jordanus takes the opposite position and argues that by 'the understanding of the word-form' (*intellectus vocis*) Priscian really means *modus significandi* (pp. 64–6), and hence that incompatible meanings do not interfere with *constructio*, however nonsensical the resulting constructions may be.

The answer depends, of course, on what counts as making a construction unacceptable, and on whether faults resulting from incompatible meanings are fundamentally different in nature from faults resulting from incompatible modes of signifying. The fully developed modistic position is that they are – in fact, that semantic anomalies, like truth-conditions, are the concern of logic, not grammar. Thomas of Erfurt refers to semantic well-formedness as *proprietas* and explains:

Dicendum est ergo quod congruitas et incongruitas causantur ex conformitate vel disconformitate modorum significandi, quae per se sunt de consideratione grammatici. Tamen proprietas vel improprietas sermonis causantur ex convenientia vel repugnantia significatorum specialium. Unde haec est congrua et propria, 'cappa nigra'; et haec est impropria, 'cappa categorica'; tamen utraque istarum est congrua.

Grammaticality and ungrammaticality are caused by the compatibility or incompatibility of modes of signifying, which are intrinsically the concern of the grammarian. But the semantic well-formedness or deviance of the utterance is caused by the compatibility or incompatibility of the meanings of the words. Hence 'black cape' is grammatical and semantically well-formed, and 'categorical cape' is semantically deviant; but both are grammatical.

Sed convenientia vel repugnantia significatorum specialium a grammatico per se non consideratur, sed magis a logico; ergo congruitas vel incongruitas in sermone non ab his causantur. (*Grammatica speculativa*, p. 304)[24]

But the compatibility or incompatibility of the specific meanings of the words is not the concern of the grammarian, but rather of the logician; hence it is not the cause of grammaticality or ungrammaticality.

Given such a distinction between grammaticality and semantic well-formedness, one can hold that syntax per se is a matter of grammaticality only, and hence that the *principia constructionis* do not include meaning. This is the position of most of the Modistae and their immediate predecessors, from Magister Jordanus (as already noted) and Pseudo-Kilwardby (pp. 93–5) to Martin of Dacia (pp. 86–7), Boethius Dacus (pp. 82–4), Michael of Marbais (Thurot 1868:223), and the late Parisian circle that includes Thomas of Erfurt (just cited), Siger de Courtrai (p. 42), and Radulphus Brito (I.16–17, pp. 140–51). A minority of Modistae, however, side with Petrus Helias and say that the *principia constructionis* also involve meaning – to be specific, that the modes of signifying are the formal cause of construction and the meaning is its material cause. Among those who hold this position are Johannes Dacus (p. 223) and Pseudo-Albertus (*Quaestiones* 10, p. 56).

Either way, the modes of signifying are indispensable in making possible the expression of compound concepts. This makes them *rationes con-*

significandi in another sense than that mentioned above – for in addition to representing Aristotle's προσσημαίνειν, *consignificare* is the standard Latin translation of Apollonius' term συσσημαίνειν and in this sense means 'have meaning in context', 'function as part of a meaningful structure' or the like. The Modistae conflated the two senses of *consignificare* gracefully by making *modi significandi* the explanatory principle of both.

However, not every mode of signifying is a *principium constructionis* – some modes, such as verb tense, are quite irrelevant to syntax. The Modistae tried, ultimately without success, to find a principled explanation of why this was so. One hypothesis that seemed promising was that only the *modi accidentales respectivi* were *principia constructionis*. This is the position of Thomas of Erfurt. It leads to an obvious difficulty: some constructions, such as that of verb plus adverb, involve no concord and hence no *modi respectivi* (in the original sense of the term), yet all constructions have to have *principia* of some sort. Thomas salvages his position by including grammatical dependency relationships among the *modi respectivi*[25] and by referring to the full sets of well-formedness conditions on constructions as *principia congruitatis* rather than *principia constructionis*. Many of the other Modistae are content with a weaker form of the same hypothesis: the respective modes are in some sense the *principia constructionis* par excellence (*maxime, immediate* or the like), while the essential modes are *principia constructionis* on a more remote level. This is the position of Boethius Dacus (pp. 107–8, 216–17) and Michael of Marbais (Thurot 1868:224), among others. In any case, everyone agrees that *modi accidentales respectivi* are always *principia constructionis*, and that *modi accidentales absoluti* never are; it is the position of the *modi essentiales* that remains in dispute.[26]

3.3 Modistic syntax: a preview

Before dealing with the major concepts of modistic syntax one by one, it will be helpful to give an overview of the complete system as summarized concisely and thoroughly in the *Grammatica speculativa* of Thomas of Erfurt. Practically all the points raised in this section will reappear, and be dealt with more thoroughly, in Chapters 4 and 5.[27]

The formation of sentences that express compound concepts is divided into three successive stages (*passiones sermonis*, 'things undergone by speech'): *constructio*, the establishment of linkages between words, *congruitas*, the application of well-formedness conditions to these linkages, and *perfectio*, the final well-formedness condition that checks whether what has been formed is a complete sentence. As in modern generative grammar, the strict separation and ordering of the three components of the grammar is meant to bring out generalizations about the structure of the language, but not necessarily to specify the actual order in which operations are carried out in the speaker's mind.

Constructio is defined in modistic grammar as the linking of one word with another. That is, in modistic grammar there is no constituent structure; no grammatical relation ever refers to a group of words taken as a unit. This means that the tree diagrams used in modern immediate constituent analysis and transformational grammar are unsuitable for representing modistic analyses. As shown in (1) below, a constituency tree for the sentence *Socrates albus currit bene* ('White Socrates runs well', one of Thomas's standard examples)[28] shows *Socrates* linked with *albus* to form a noun phrase, *currit* linked with *bene* to form a verb phrase, and *Socrates albus* linked with *currit bene* to form a sentence.

(1)

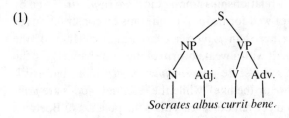

Socrates albus currit bene.

'White Socrates runs well.'

Modistic theory presupposes that the last-mentioned of these linkages is impossible; *constructio* always connects a single word to another single word, never a group to a group. Hence, in the modistic analysis, the subject–verb relation is expressed by linking *Socrates* to *currit*. (Both analyses link *Socrates* with *albus*, and *currit* with *bene*.) The modistic analysis, shown in (2), is essentially that proposed by modern dependency grammarians, who share with the Modistae the assumption that grammatical relations link individual words (see for example Tesnière 1959 and, for comparison of several approaches, Bauer 1979).

(2)

Socrates albus currit bene.

'White Socrates runs well.'

Thomas's complete classification of constructions is shown in Figure 3. Each two-word construction is classified as transitive or intransitive depending on whether the two words in it pertain to the same real-world referent. For instance, *Socrates albus*, 'white Socrates', and *Socrates currit*, 'Socrates runs', are intransitive constructions, since each of them makes or entails a statement solely about Socrates. By contrast, *filius Socratis*, 'the son of Socrates', is a transitive construction, since the son and Socrates are distinct individuals; so is *videt Platonem*, 'sees Plato', since Plato is distinct from the person who sees him (and to whom the verb principally refers). Of course, the entities involved do not have to be human beings. *Liber philosophiae*, 'book of philosophy', is a transitive construction, since the book and the philosophy are conceived of and signified as separate entities, while *liber philosophicus*, 'philosophical book', is intransitive, since in it, philosophy is conceived of not as an entity, but as an attribute of something else. What counts is the *modus significandi*, not the *significatum*.

Cross-cutting the transitive–intransitive distinction is the distinction between *constructiones personarum*, which do not involve the relation of main verb to subject or object, and *constructiones actuum*, which do. The origin of this terminology is connected with Priscian's concept of *transitio personarum*, 'change of referent' (see section 2.1 above). The speculative grammarians noticed that in a construction involving a main verb and its object, there is not merely change of referent, but transfer of action (*transitio actuum*) as well: in *videt Platonem*, the action of seeing 'goes across' to Plato from the person who sees him. Correspondingly, in the relation of the verb to its subject, as in *Socrates videt*, there is 'non-transfer of action' (*intransitio actuum*); the person who does the seeing is the same as the person signified by the subject. In certain constructions involving no verb, such as *filius Socratis*, there is *transitio personarum* without *transitio actuum*; and in others, such as *Socrates albus*, there is *intransitio personarum*, no change of referent at all. Hence a construction can be *transitiva actuum*, *transitiva personarum*, *intransitiva actuum*, or *intransitiva personarum*.[29]

Within each construction there are two grammatical relations, that of *primum* to *secundum* and that of *dependens* to *terminans*. As I shall argue in detail in section 4.4, the *primum–secundum* relation is very similar to what modern theoreticians call dependency: the *secundum* presupposes the presence of the *primum*. In modern terms, the *primum* and *secundum* are head and modifier, respectively. Borrowing the diagrammatic conventions of present-day dependency grammar, and representing each *primum* node

38

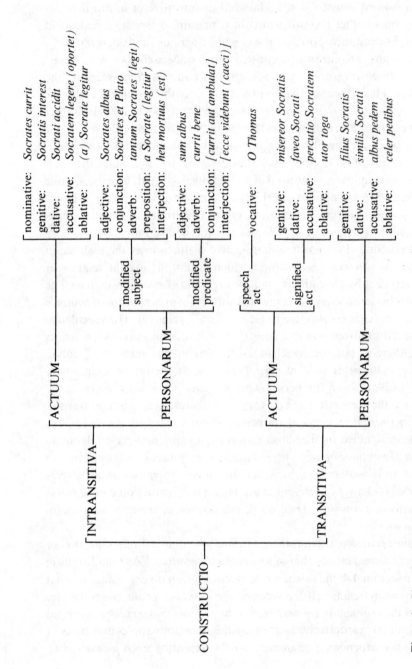

Figure 3. Classification of constructions (Thomas of Erfurt).
Parenthesized words are not part of the construction in question but are included to provide context. The examples are Thomas's except for those in square brackets, which I have supplied. Some of these constructions are problematic; the problems that they raise are dealt with in Chapters 4 and 5.

higher than the *secundum* to which it is connected, we can represent Thomas's favorite example sentence as follows:

(3)

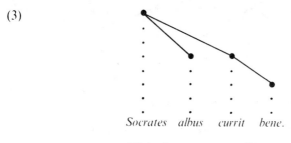

Socrates albus currit bene.

'White Socrates runs well.'

The subject is the head of the sentence because, in Aristotelian ontology, substance, which is consignified by the noun, is prior to predication, which is consignified by the verb. The verb is then a modifier of the subject; *albus* is straightforwardly a modifier of *Socrates*, and *bene* a modifier of *currit*. (In order to fit the whole range of constructions into the head–modifier mold, Thomas treats prepositions as markers that serve the function of extra noun cases and hence are modifiers of nouns. Conjunctions are difficult to fit into the system at all; the special problems that they raise will be considered in section 5.1.)

As I shall show in section 4.4, the *dependens–terminans* relation is simply an extension of Petrus Helias' concept of referentially defined *regimen*, though the Modistae are by no means explicit in recognizing it as such. The clearest thing Thomas says about it is that in transitive constructions the *primum–secundum* and *dependens–terminans* relations run in the same direction (that is, the *primum* is the *dependens* and the *secundum* is the *terminans*), while in intransitive constructions the two relations run in opposite directions. From this it follows that if a construction introduces a new referent through the *secundum*, the constructible with the new referent – the *secundum* – is the *terminans*, while if it does not, then the *primum* is the *terminans*, since it establishes the referent to which the *secundum* applies. That is, Thomas applies the notion of co-reference not just to nouns and pronouns, but to all the words in the sentence; the *terminans* of a construction establishes the referent to which the whole construction (or at least the word that the construction introduces) applies.

This can be illustrated by diagramming a sentence in the same manner as above and adding arrowheads that point from *dependens* to *terminans*:[30]

(4)

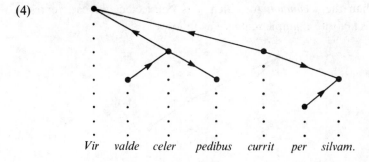

Vir   valde   celer   pedibus   currit   per   silvam.

'A man truly swift on his feet runs through the forest.'

The arrowheads converge on the words that refer to distinct entities in the real world – 'man', 'feet', and 'forest' – showing that each of these is a *terminans* on which the reference of other sentence elements depends.

4 *Syntactic structure*

The great achievement of the Modistae with regard to syntactic theory was the development of a formal model of sentence structure. In the fully developed modistic model, the sentence was analyzed into a set of 'constructions,' or linkages connecting one word with another, and each construction was then described in terms of the two primitive grammatical relations, that of *dependens* to *terminans* and that of *primum* to *secundum*. The emergence of this model marked the culmination of the move toward formally explicit, conceptually parsimonious syntactic descriptions that had been going on since the early days of *regimen*-theory.

In many ways the syntactic theory of the Modistae reflects the Aristotelian philosophical paradigm within which they worked; medieval philosophers regularly drew on the ontology and metaphysics of Aristotle for the kind of tools of thought that modern linguists draw from set theory and related disciplines. For example, the one-to-one relationship of *dependens* to *terminans* in each construction lent itself well to treatment in terms of Aristotelian dichotomies such as matter–form and actual–potential, and it may be that this fact helped promote the idea that all constructions should in fact be viewed as one-to-one relationships.

However, it would be a mistake to think of modistic grammar as a force-fit of linguistic structure onto Aristotelian metaphysics. The Modistae, being realists, held that the perceptible world had a definite structure and that the semantic function of language was to represent this structure; hence they used Aristotelian ontology as a theory of the things language could signify, and as such it figured prominently in their semantics. But they cited Aristotle only on general matters of ontology and logic; their authority on grammar, whom they viewed with a certain amount of healthy skepticism, was Priscian. Particularly in the works of sophisticated grammarians such as Martin of Dacia, the appeals to Aristotle served either to provide standardized ways of dividing up complex subject matter, or to supply tests of the logical coherence of theoretical claims; and in the case of *quaestiones disputatae*, irrelevant or intentionally misapplied quotations from Aristotle were a standard source of straw-man arguments for refutation.[1]

4.1 Construction

The first principle that the modistic syntacticians had to establish was that it in fact made sense to describe all constructions (and not just many or most constructions) as linkages joining two and only two words. This involved a shift in the meaning of 'construction'. For Priscian, *constructio* had meant simply 'syntactic structure' and had referred, as often as not, to the whole sentence.[2] Further, many medieval grammarians altered Priscian's definition of the sentence 'oratio est ordinatio dictionum congrua' ('A sentence is a well-formed arrangement of words', II.15), by changing the first word to *constructio*; among those who quote the definition in the altered form are Hugh of St Victor, Petrus Helias, Johannes le Rus, and Martin of Dacia.[3] From this it is clear that *constructio* could still mean 'sentence' in the time of the Modistae.

On the other hand, Priscian's frequent statements that one word 'requires' or 'is construed with' another, together with the theory of *regimen* that developed out of them, inclined grammarians to view sentence structure as a set of word-to-word linkages. So did the tendency to classify constructions as transitive or intransitive. Sponcius Provincialis, a didactic grammarian writing in 1242, senses the tension between the two views:

Scias igitur quod 'constructio' dicitur in grammatica tribus modis. Dicitur constructio actio constituentis, de quo actu vel de qua actione nihil ad praesens. Et dicitur constructio tota oratio stricte constituta, hoc est ex dictionibus composita, sicut cum dicitur 'P. legit Lucanum', et secundum istum modum constructio definitur sic: 'Constructio est congrua dictionum ordinatio congruam sententiam perfectamque

You should know, then, that the term 'construction' is used in three different ways in grammar.
(1) The act of composing a sentence is called construction; about this we have nothing to say at present.
(2) 'Construction' is also the term for the whole sentence in the strict sense, i.e., the aggregate of words, such as 'P[etrus] reads Lucan', and in this sense construction is defined as 'a grammatical arrangement of words manifesting

demonstrans' ... et dividitur in quattuor partes, transitivam, intransitivam, reciprocam et retransitivam constructionem, de quibus ponemus descriptionem inferius, et doctrinam. Tertio modo dicitur constructio modus construendi, scilicet quemadmodum una dictio dicitur construi cum alia transitive vel intransitive ... (Fierville 1886:177–8)

a coherent and complete thought' and is divided into four classes, transitive, intransitive, reciprocal, and retransitive, concerning which we shall give our description and doctrine below.
(3) 'Construction' is the term for the way words are put together. In this sense a word is said to be joined to another word transitively or intransitively.

Among the Modistae, Martin of Dacia still evinces some uncertainty on this point; he speaks of construction as the joining of a single *dependens* to a single *terminans* (pp. 88–9) but then refers to the whole sentence as a *constructio* that has a single *primum constructibile* (pp. 91–2). The later Modistae, however, insist on using *constructio* exclusively to refer to the union of two individual constructibles.

Radulphus Brito devotes a whole question to this point (I.8, 'Utrum constructio fiat solum ex duobus constructibilibus': 'Whether a construction is formed out of two and only two elements'). He addresses the issue by examining structures of more than two words that do not appear to be decomposable into two-word linkages; the best examples are *vado ad ecclesiam*, 'I go to church', and *annulus ex auro*, 'a ring of gold', in which the preposition appears to be a *medium construendi*, an intermediary effecting the linkage of *vado* to *ecclesiam* and of *annulus* to *auro*. Radulphus deals with these apparent counterexamples to the two-word principle by arguing that the preposition is in fact more closely associated with its object than with the verb or noun that precedes it. He concludes that the preposition should be treated as a modifier of its object, rather than as a *medium construendi*. It is not perfectly clear whether he holds that the preposition–object relation is itself a *constructio* or something else (a matter of morphology in which the preposition is a separable marker, perhaps).[4] Thomas of Erfurt, however, explicitly lists the preposition among the types of noun modifiers that participate in *constructio intransitiva personarum* (*Grammatica speculativa*, p. 292).

There are, then, no constructions comprising more than two words, but are there any that comprise fewer than two? Radulphus considers instances of what seem to be constructions consisting of a single word, either because the word contains more than one meaningful element (*im-pius*, *armi-ger*) or because it functions as a complete sentence (as in response to a question: *quid est summum bonum? honestas*). He says that even structurally complex words, such as *impius*, refer to single concepts and hence do not involve syntactic combination, which would entail the union of separate ideas;[5] although he does not quite say so, he doubtless has in mind the fact that speakers for the most part draw their words (including compound words) from an established repertoire, while they create new sentences afresh on the spot.[6] As for the one-word answers to questions, he refers to his own Questions I.30 to 33, where he deals with verbs that have understood subjects (*curro*, 'I run' = *ego curro*, and the like); the implication is that in all one-word sentences a subject and a predicate are understood, even if only the most salient word is actually uttered.

4.2 Transitivity

If each construction comprises two and only two words, then every construction is either transitive or intransitive – i.e., either contains a *transitio personarum* or does not – and Priscian's other two types, reciprocal and retransitive, can be dispensed with by defining them as combinations of simpler constructions. This is implicitly the view of Hugh of St Victor,[7] who does not appear to consider it a novelty, though Petrus Helias, writing some years later, has not yet accepted it and argues for keeping the four-class system (pp. 43–4).

Applying the criterion of *transitio personarum* to individual constructions raised a problem that was first fully addressed, as far as we know, by Martin of Dacia. A sentence with a transitive verb, such as 'Socrates reads Vergil', is obviously transitive, taken as a whole; 'Socrates' and 'Vergil' are distinct individuals. But which of its two constituent constructions is the transitive one, 'Socrates + reads' or 'reads + Vergil'? That is, should the verb be treated as co-referent with the subject or the object?

Traditionally, 'Socrates reads' would be analyzed as intransitive, by analogy to similar constructions with intransitive verbs ('Socrates runs'), and 'reads Vergil' would be analyzed as transitive. This is the treatment presented, for instance, by Petrus Helias (p. 44). But Martin points out that the traditional definitions of 'transitive' and 'intransitive' provide no justification for such an analysis: the action of the verb is at least as inherent in the object as in the subject – more so, in fact, if one accepts the conceptual analysis of action in Aristotle's *Physics* – and hence there is no reason to identify the verb solely with the subject. He explains:

Constructionis secundum omnes grammaticos haec est prima divisio, quod constructionum alia est transitiva, alia intransitiva. Ad has duas reducuntur omnes speciales constructiones. Ergo de his consequenter videndum est quid sit constructio transitiva et quid intransitiva, et quomodo quaelibet illarum in speciales constructiones dividatur. Iuxta quod primo est notandum quod de constructione transitiva et intransitiva secundum hunc modum fit et semper fuerat sermo quod, cum omnis constructio aut est transitiva aut intransitiva, aut ergo constructibilia sic se habent quod ipsa denotantur per suos modos significandi unum et idem alteri, et sic est constructio intransitiva – dicitur enim constructio intransitiva esse in qua dictiones positae pertinent ad eandem personam vel rem vel ut ad eandem – aut ipsa constructibilia sic se habent quod denotantur unum ut diversum alteri seu diversum ab altero, et sic est constructio transitiva – dicitur enim transitiva in qua dictiones positae pertinent ad diversas personas vel ut ad diversas.

According to all grammarians, the most important classification of constructions is that some are transitive and some intransitive; all the other subclassifications reduce to those two. Therefore we must next examine what a transitive or intransitive construction is, and how each of these is subdivided into more specific types. In this connection, the first thing to note is that it is and always has been said, concerning transitive and intransitive constructions, that, since every construction is either transitive or intransitive, the constructibles therefore are related in either of two ways: either such that, by virtue of their modes of signifying, the things denoted by them are one and the same, and thus the construction is intransitive – for the intransitive construction is said to be the one in which the words pertain to the same person or thing or have the effect of pertaining to the same person or thing – or else in such a way that one thing is denoted as distinct from the other, and thus the construction is transitive – for the transitive construction is said to be the one in which the words pertain to different persons or have the effect of so doing.

Salva reverentia ita dicentium illud non videtur valere, quia cum dicitur 'constructio intransitiva est quando unum constructibilium dependet ad alterum ut idem sibi,' hoc non est verum. Si enim hoc esset verum, sequeretur quod omnis constructio esset intransitiva, quod est impossibile. Non enim est possibile dividens cum diviso converti. Quod autem hoc sequeretur, evidens est, quia in omni constructione unum constructibile dependet ad aliud ut idem sibi ut patet in constructione quae maxime est transitiva ... ut cum dicitur 'percutio Socratem'; 'percutio' enim dependet ad 'Socratem' ut idem sibi. Magis enim est actio idem passo quam agenti, cum in omni passo sit sicut in subiecto, quia actio et passio unus motus sunt et sunt in patiente ut in subiecto. Ergo et cetera.
(*Modi significandi*, pp. 89–90)

With all due respect to those who say this, it does not seem to be valid, since when it is said that 'the construction is intransitive when one of the constructibles depends on the other as on something identical to itself,' this is not true. If it were true, it would follow that every construction would be intransitive, which is impossible – the subclassification cannot be interchanged with the thing it subclassifies. That this would follow is evident, since in *every* construction one constructible depends on the other as on something identical with itself. This is apparent even in the transitive construction par excellence, as in 'I hit Socrates'; for 'hit' depends on 'Socrates' as on something identical with itself. The reason is that the action is more to be identified with the one that undergoes it than with the one that brings it about, since action and passion are one motion and are attributes of the thing that undergoes it.

The solution Martin proposes is to keep the traditional analysis but change the definitions of *constructio transitiva* and *intransitiva*. Instead of appealing to co-reference directly, he proposes to define 'transitive' and 'intransitive' in terms of two other grammatical relations, *primum–secundum* and *dependens–terminans*. Before examining the details of Martin's proposal it will be necessary to look at the complete modistic theory of grammatical relations.

4.3 *Regimen* in modistic grammar

Because of its extensive treatment in didactic grammars, the concept of *regimen* was familiar to every medieval schoolboy; but insofar as the Modistae use it, they do so without resolving any of the controversies that had attended its use since the twelfth century.

In the pre-modistic period, Magister Jordanus takes pains to distinguish between Petrus Helias' referential concept of government (which he calls *exigentia*) and the more widely used morphological definition, for which he reserves the term *regimen*;[8] but then, as Sirridge (1980:xxi) observes, he 'tends to forget his own distinction.' Simon Dacus Domifex refers to both relations as *regimen* and seems not to be fully aware that they are different. His first definition, '*Regimen* is the voluntary joining of words on the basis of the compatibility of what they signify or consignify,'[9] is neutral between the two approaches; his use of terms from didactic grammar such as *regere ex vi* is reminiscent of the morphological criterion; and he cites Petrus Helias extensively, not only for the referential definition of *regimen*, but also for some statements, such as 'regens debet esse formale' and 'regimen ... est formatio dictionis cum dictione' (p. 55), that do not occur in Petrus' section on *regimen*, and even for one, 'regere nihil aliud est quam significationem suam alteri accommodare' (p. 58), that represents exactly the thesis that Petrus attacks. Johannes le Rus eschews *regimen* altogether and states his description in terms of *determinatio*.[10]

Among the available writings of the Modistae proper, the only substantial discussion of *regimen* is that by Petrus Croccus, who in writing a commentary on the *Doctrinale* could hardly have avoided the topic. In his question 'Utrum regimen sit possibile' he cites a definition of *regimen* resembling Petrus Helias' referential definition, rejects it, offers the morphological definition as an alternative, explains that not all constructions involve *regimen*, and proceeds to handle several standard questions such as *quid sit causa constructionis*.[11] It is obvious that *constructio* is the theoretical concept he is really interested in developing, and his brief discussion of the morphological definition of *regimen* is meant only to explain the use of the term in the *Doctrinale*.

Simon Dacus Modista and Anonymus Norimbergensis mention *regimen* occasionally, particularly in their discussions of the ablative absolute (which is supposed to be *absolutus a regimine*); they hold to the morphological definition and do not even mention alternatives.[12] Siger de Courtrai has a distinctive idea of *regimen* which he unfortunately never quite makes clear: he accepts traditional morphological *regimen* as far as it goes but argues that it is inadequate because it leaves out concord (e.g., *Socrates albus*) and relationships involving indeclinables (e.g., *O magister*).[13] Radulphus Brito uses *regere* once, as a synonym for *exigere* (I.6, p. 111); Martin of Dacia and Thomas of Erfurt do not use the term at all, even though they were surely familiar with it from their schooldays.

4.4 *Dependens* and *terminans*

One of the basic principles of modistic syntax is that the relation between the two words in a *constructio* is not symmetrical; one of the words is identified as *dependens* and the other as *terminans*. But the Modistae never say exactly what this *dependens–terminans* relation consists in. The only definition of it that Thomas of Erfurt gives is a metaphysical one:[14]

Sicut ex materia et forma, quorum unum est in actu, alterum vero in potentia, fit per se compositum in natura, sic ex ratione dependendi et terminandi fit per se constructio in sermone. Illud autem constructibile est dependens, quod ratione alicuius modi significandi terminum petit vel exigit; illud vero constructibile est terminans, quod ratione alicuius modi significandi terminum dat vel concedit. (*Grammatica speculativa*, p. 280)

Just as a composite entity in nature consists of matter and form, of which one is actual and the other is potential, in the same way construction in language comes about through the exerting and fulfilling of dependencies. The dependent constructible is the one that by virtue of some mode of signifying seeks or requires a terminus to fulfill its dependency; the terminant is the constructible that by virtue of some mode of signifying gives or supplies that terminus.

Indeed, Martin of Dacia leaves the *dependens–terminans* relation completely undefined even though it is a crucial part of the new theory of transitivity that he is presenting; he assumes that the difference between *dependens* and *terminans* is intuitively obvious to his readers. His assumption appears to be justified; the Modistae rarely or never disagree as to which is which.

Yet modern scholars have found the nature of the *dependens–terminans* relation far from obvious (cf. Bursill-Hall 1971:311–12, Pinborg 1973,

Covington 1979, and Percival [to appear]). The relation itself is indicated by arrows pointing from *dependens* to *terminans* in the following examples (which are taken from Thomas of Erfurt):

(1)   Intransitive constructions:

(a)   *Socrates legit*   'Socrates reads'

(b)   *a Socrate*   'from Socrates'

(c)   *Socrates albus*   'white Socrates'

(d)   *currit bene*   'runs well'

(e)   *est albus*   'is white'

(f)   *Socrates et Plato*   'Socrates and Plato'

(2)   Transitive constructions:

(a)   *legit Vergilium*   'reads Vergil'

(b)   *filius Socratis*   'son of Socrates'

(c)   *similis Socrati*   'similar to Socrates'

The arrows correspond to no grammatical relation recognized by modern theory. They do not represent dependency in the modern sense, since the arrow points toward the head noun in *Socrates albus* but away from it in *filius Socratis*. Nor is the relation one of morphological government, for sometimes the *dependens* determines the form of the *terminans* (as in *legit Vergilium*) and sometimes the opposite is the case (as in *Socrates albus*).

Thomas's remarks about form and matter are suggestive, especially since other Modistae make similar statements. To quote, for example, Simon Dacus Modista:

Constructibile dependens est in potentia, quia habet se sicut materia, et constructibile terminans est in actu, quia habet se sicut forma. (*Quaestiones*, p. 112)

The dependent constructible is potential, since it plays the role of matter, and the terminant constructible is actual, since it plays the role of form.

Can we, then, conclude (with Bursill-Hall 1966, 1972:107) that since the *terminans* is the 'form' of the construction, it must be the constructible that determines the construction-type – that is, the one from which the construction-type can more easily be inferred? Unfortunately, no; such a principle would be hard if not impossible to apply in practice. If anything, it is the *dependens* that varies more from one type of construction to another (cf. Covington 1979:474); the *terminans* is almost always a noun. The remarks about matter and form seem in fact to be an explication of the concept of dependency, and not a practical criterion for doing grammatical analyses; that no great weight is to be given to the matter–form analogy is shown by the fact that Radulphus Brito gets it the other way around, identifying matter with the *terminans* and form with the *dependens*.[15]

The key to the puzzle is to be found rather in a remark made by Petrus Croccus at the end of the section on *regimen* in his *Doctrinale* commentary:

Superius egit auctor de causis constructionis sive de principiis sive dependentiis per quas dependentias, id est per quos modos significandi dependentes, ista constructibilia regunt alia constructibilia terminantia eorum dependentias. (fol. 108va)	Above, the author dealt with the causes of construction – that is, the principles or dependencies by means of which dependencies or dependent modes of signifying the constructibles govern other constructibles that terminate their dependencies.

That is, the governing element is the *dependens*, and the governed element is the *terminans*[16] – the *dependens–terminans* relationship is nothing other than *regimen*. But what kind of *regimen* is Petrus referring to? Not the morphological government treated in the *Doctrinale* itself, since some of the modistic examples of *dependens* and *terminans*, such as *currit bene*, do not involve morphology at all.

On the other hand, the referential *regimen* of Petrus Helias can be extended to cover the full range of *dependens–terminans* relations without difficulty; in every case the *dependens* lacks a referent and the *terminans* supplies it. For example, the verb, which stands for a property or relation, depends on its subject and object to designate the entities that the property or relation pertains to; hence the verb is *dependens* and the subject and object are *terminans* of their respective constructions. The situation is even clearer with the preposition, which by itself signifies pure relation ('in', 'on', 'to', 'from') and depends on its object to indicate what entity the relation applies to. The same holds for a relational adjective like 'similar', which depends on its complement. This much Petrus Helias had already established a century earlier (cf. section 2.3 above), and the development of the concept of *suppositio* in medieval logic had given strength to the idea that only things, and not predicates or relations, can be referents in the strict sense. (Something similar is still with us in first-order predicate logic, which divides the universe of discourse into individuals and predicates.)

Extending the *dependens–terminans* relation, thus defined, to constructions that do not involve *regimen* is equally straightforward. For instance, in *Socrates albus*, 'white Socrates', the adjective 'white' lacks a referent because it signifies a property, while the noun 'Socrates', which signifies an entity, has one; hence the adjective depends on the noun. Likewise, in *Socrates et Plato* the conjunction *et* has no referent; it expresses a relation between *Socrates* and *Plato* and hence depends on both of them for reference. (Two *constructiones* are of course involved, *Socrates* and *et* and *et* and *Plato*.)

The case of *filius Socratis* is a bit more difficult, since *filius* already has a referent, or seems to, and therefore ought not to depend on another noun. Petrus Helias, noticing this difficulty, had argued that in a construction such as this, *filius* actually signifies a relation, not an individual, and hence the referential dependency does exist. This is reasonable as far as it goes, but, as Simon Dacus Modista notes, kinship terms are not the only nouns that govern genitives. It is plausible to say that 'son' expresses a relation, but in a construction like *cappa Socratis*, 'Socrates' cape', does 'cape' likewise stand for a relation rather than an individual entity? After considering the matter carefully, Simon answers that it does – that there is an element of relation in the meaning of *cappa* in this construction even though *cappa* ordinarily signifies a thing.[17]

Finally, there are constructions, such as *est albus* and *currit bene*, in which neither of the constructibles has a referent; but one of them comes nearer to having a referent than the other, and hence the *dependens–terminans* relation can still be applied to them. For example, in *est albus*, 'is white', neither 'is' nor 'white' has a referent, but 'is' has a way of obtaining a referent – through the construction that links it to the subject of the sentence – and hence 'is' depends on the subject and 'white' depends on 'is'. Similarly, in 'runs well', 'runs' depends on the subject and 'well' depends on 'runs'. The establishment of reference in these examples takes place mediately rather than immediately, but it is still clear in which direction the *dependens–terminans* relation has to run.

4.5 *Primum* and *secundum*

The *dependens–terminans* relation is one of the two things Martin of Dacia needs in order to state his new definition of transitivity; the other is the concept of *primum constructibile*. For Martin, there is only one *primum constructibile* in the whole sentence – the subject – and all the other words are *posteriora constructibilia* (p. 91). Given these presuppositions, he defines transitive and intransitive construction as follows:

Tunc accipio ... quod in omni constructione non sunt plures modi significandi in genere dependentium quam duo: aut modus significandi quo aliquid dependet ad primum constructibile (vel ad aliquid quod dependentiam habet ulteriorem ad primum constructibile – et hoc est dictum quod iste modus significandi talis est quod ipse dependet ad primum constructibile vel mediate vel immediate), aut est modus significandi dependentis quo aliquod constructibile non dependet ad primum constructibile nec mediate nec immediate.

Then I accept that in every construction there are no more than two kinds of dependent mode of signifying: either a mode of signifying by which something depends on the *primum constructibile* (or on something that ultimately depends on the *primum* – I say this because the mode of signifying is such that it depends on the *primum* either mediately or immediately), or a mode of signifying on the part of a *dependens* whereby there is a constructible that does not depend on the *primum* either mediately or immediately.

Tunc dico quod primus istorum duorum modorum est principium tantum intransitivae constructionis, secundus vero est principium transitivae constructionis, ita tamen quod constructio intransitiva est simplex vel in suo genere, quoniam omnis dependentia in huiusmodi constructione vadit ad primum constructibile vel mediate vel immediate. Immediate, ut 'homo albus' sive 'homo currit' – in his

Then I say that the first of these two modes is the defining principle only of intransitive construction, and the second is the defining principle of transitive construction – but in such a way that the intransitive construction is a simple entity in a class by itself, since in such a construction every dependency goes back to the *primum* either mediately or immediately. Immediately, as in *homo albus* or *homo currit* – for in

enim constructionibus
dependentiae terminantur ad
primum constructibile – unde hoc
quod est 'albus' immediate
dependet ad hominem, et hoc
quod est 'currit' eodem modo.

Similiter dependet aliquod
constructibile mediate ut patet
cum dicitur 'homo currit bene':
hoc quod est 'bene' per se
dependet ad hoc quod est 'currit'
tanquam ad suum proprium
determinabile per se, cum
adverbium sit vi verbi adiectivum;
hoc autem quod est 'currit'
dependentiam habet ad primum
constructibile, et ideo hoc quod est
'bene' dependet ad hoc quod est
'homo', sed hoc est mediante
verbo. Propter hoc dicimus hanc
constructionem esse intransitivam
simpliciter ut cum dicitur 'homo
albus currit bene'; hic enim omnis
dependentia vadit ad primum
constructibile vel mediate vel
immediate. Sed haec 'homo albus'
vel 'homo currit' intransitiva est in
suo genere. Propter hoc diximus
supra secundum hunc modum,
constructionem esse intransitivam
simpliciter vel in suo genere.
(pp. 91–2)

Modus autem quo aliquid
dependet ad aliud a primo
constructibili, dummodo nec
mediate nec immediate vadat ad
primum constructibile, et modus
terminantis in alio a primo

these constructions the
dependencies are fulfilled by the
primum constructibile, and hence
albus depends immediately on
homo, and so does *currit*.

Likewise, a constructible can
depend on the *primum* mediately,
as in *homo currit bene*; here *bene*
in itself depends on *currit* as the
thing that it modifies, since the
adverb is in effect the adjective of
the verb; but *currit* depends on the
primum constructibile, and hence
bene depends on *homo* with the
verb as intermediary. This is why
we say that this construction,
homo albus currit bene, is
intransitive as a whole, for in it
every dependency goes back to the
primum constructibile either
mediately or immediately. But
homo albus or *homo currit* is
intransitive only as a unit. For this
reason we said above that a
construction could be intransitive
either as a whole or as a unit, or
both.

But the mode whereby something
depends on something other than
the *primum*, while the dependency
does not go back to the *primum*
either mediately or immediately,
and the mode whereby a

constructibili, principia	dependency is terminated in
constructionis transitivae sunt.	something other than the *primum*
(p. 93)	– these are the modes that define a
	transitive construction.

The new definition gives the desired result: in a sentence like

(3)

Socrates videt Platonem.
(*primum*)

'Socrates sees Plato.'

the construction *Socrates videt* is clearly intransitive, since the dependency goes back to the *primum*, while *videt Platonem* is clearly transitive, since in it, the dependency is terminated by something distinct from the *primum*. Martin has successfully eliminated the problem of deciding whether the verb is co-referential with the subject or the object; he looks not at co-reference itself, but at the direction of dependency relationships.

It is not entirely clear where Martin gets his idea of *primum constructibile*. The closest antecedent I have been able to find is the term *primo constructibile* used by Roger Bacon (*Summa grammatica*, pp. 33–5). Bacon makes much of the idea, common in medieval grammar, that the structure of a sentence is like a physical motion (a *motus*, perhaps originally identified with *transitio personarum*) that begins at the subject and proceeds through the verb to the object or complement.[18] The *primo constructibile* is then simply the starting point of the motion. Even without the *motus* analogy, there are reasons for viewing the subject as 'first constructible': it is usually the first word in the sentence; being a noun, it comes first in the *ordo naturalis* of the parts of speech; and, representing a substance rather than a property, it is logically presupposed by the rest of the sentence. Priscian makes it quite clear that, in some informal way, he considers the nominative subject (or the vocative, which for him is the subject of the imperative) to be the fixed starting point of the sentence:

Nominativus et vocativus absoluti	The nominative and vocative are
sunt, id est, per unam personam	independent – that is, they can be
intransitive possunt proferri, ut ...	used to refer to one person with no
'Aristoteles disputat'. (XVIII.2)	change of referent, as in 'Aristotle
	debates'.

Et attendendum quod	And note that the nominative that
nominativus, qui verbo adiungitur,	is joined to the verb remains as a
immobilis casus ipse manet et vel	fixed, unchanging case, and has
nullum vel eum solum assumit	added to it only the oblique case
alterius casus obliquum, qui verbo	form that is governed by the verb,
construitur. (XVIII.35)	or none at all.

Hence Martin's concept of *primum constructibile* has a Priscianic basis.

However, the Modistae soon replaced Martin's model, in which the subject of the sentence was the only *primum*, with a model that identified a *primum* and a *secundum* in each individual construction. Pinborg (1973) has suggested that the reason for the change was that Martin's model gave the wrong result in dealing with modifiers of the object. Consider the sentence:

(4)

Socrates senex saepe videt iuvenem Platonem.
(*primum*)

'Old Socrates often sees young Plato.'

Martin's criterion entails that a construction is intransitive if and only if, beginning with that construction's dependency arrow, it is possible to follow the arrows ('mediately or immediately') back to the *primum constructibile*. By this criterion, *Socrates senex* and *Socrates videt* are obviously intransitive, since their arrows point directly to the *primum*; *saepe videt* is also intransitive, though to get back to the *primum* it is necessary to follow two arrows in succession; and *videt Platonem* is transitive, since its arrow points away from the *primum*. So far so good; but what about *Platonem iuvenem*? According to Martin's criterion, this is a transitive construction, since there is no path from it back to the *primum* (the path is blocked by the rightward-pointing arrow of *videt Platonem*); yet *Platonem iuvenem* is exactly the same kind of construction as *Socrates senex*, which Martin's test (along with every authority since Priscian) has labeled intransitive. This is not a satisfactory result, and a modification is obviously called for.[19]

The modification that was made, and which Thomas of Erfurt describes most clearly, involved identifying each construction's *primum* and *secundum* by the following criteria:

Illud est in omni constructione constructibile primum, quod post se dependet ad obliquum; illud vero secundum, quod ante se dependet ad suppositum. Illud est etiam secundum, quod dependet ad determinabile. Et ratio horum est, quia illud quod post se dependet ad obliquum, dependet ad ipsum ut ad terminum et ultimum; quod autem ante se dependet ad suppositum dependet ad ipsum ut ad principium et ad primum; quod autem dependet ad suum determinabile dependet ad aliquid prius se; determinatio autem, et dispositio rei, est posterior ipsa re. (*Grammatica speculativa*, p. 280)

In every construction, the *primum* is the constructible that depends on a subsequent oblique case form; the *secundum* is the one that depends on a prior subject. A constructible that depends on something that it modifies is also a *secundum*. And the reason for these facts is that anything that depends on a subsequent oblique case form depends on it as on a termination or endpoint; anything that depends on a prior subject depends on it as on a starting point or origin. A constructible that depends on something it modifies likewise depends on something prior to itself, since the modication and disposition of a thing are subsequent to the thing itself.

Identifying transitive and intransitive constructions is then a simple matter: if the *primum* depends on the *secundum*, then the construction is transitive, while if the opposite is the case, the construction is intransitive.[20]

But the criteria for identifying the *primum* and *secundum* themselves are not, at first sight, clear. To begin with, what does Thomas mean by *ante se* and *post se*? Obviously, he wants it to follow from his criteria that the verb is construed intransitively with the subject and transitively with the object; but is he identifying subject and object on the basis of word order (i.e., before or after the verb) or of something more abstract?

The answer involves the concepts of *constructio ante se* and *post se* (or *ex parte ante* and *ex parte post*) developed some time earlier and extensively used in didactic grammar. Percival (1975:234–5, 237) has argued that in certain grammatical works that stand completely outside the modistic tradition, these terms refer purely to word order; but there are grammarians who use them in ways that completely preclude such an interpretation.

The grammarians all agree that the verb is construed with the subject *ex parte ante* and with the object *ex parte post*. Since the usual word order of medieval Latin is subject, verb, object, the *ante–post* terminology matches the word order in the majority of cases; but there are exceptions. For example, Sponcius Provincialis analyzes the impersonal sentence

(5)   *Taedet animam meam vitae meae*
                          acc.   gen.

'My soul is weary of my life' (Job 10:1)

by saying that the verb *taedet* takes an accusative *ante se* and a genitive *post se*; further, in dealing with the Vulgate Bible's *in conveniendo populos in unum* (which, he explains, means 'when the peoples came together into one')[21] he says that the verb is taking an accusative *ante se*, an accusative subject like that of the infinitive. That is, in both analyses Sponcius applies *ante* to something that follows the verb in linear order.

Sponcius is no innovator, and these analyses provide strong evidence that *ante* and *post* regularly referred to the subject and object (or complement) roles, respectively, and not to the word order; it is likely that they had the same Priscianic basis as Martin's concept of the subject alone as *primum*. The Modistae retain the *ante–post* terminology and normally apply it only to the relation between the verb and its subject or complement.[22] Hence, by referring to 'subject *ante se*' and 'oblique *post se*,' Thomas definitely means that the verb is *secundum* in the subject–verb construction, and *primum* in the verb–object construction, regardless of the word order.

As for the principle that, in a construction of modifier with modified, the modifier is *secundum* and the modified element is *primum*, this follows straightforwardly from medieval ontology: modification signifies attribution, and substances are prior to their attributes. This relation can of course be the opposite of the normal word order, as in constructions such as *omnis homo*, in which the *secundum* comes first.

The idea that modifiers are in some sense logically subsequent to the words they modify had already occurred to Hugh of St Victor some two centuries earlier; he remarked:

Item quidquid in constructione	Whatever is added to the sentence
adicitur praeter nomen et verbum	besides the (main) noun and verb
vel nominis vel verbi determinatio	is apparently either a modifier of

esse videtur, cum priora sunt semper quae determinantur quam ea quibus determinamus aliquid. Itaque nomen et verbum priora esse necesse est, deinde quae determinant nomen et verbum. (*De grammatica*, p. 107)

the noun or a modifier of the verb, since things modified are always prior to the things with which we modify them. And so it is necessary that the noun and verb be prior, and then come the things that modify the noun and the verb.

He doubtless had in mind Priscian's observation that a long, elaborate sentence can be shortened word by word and will remain a sentence as long as the main noun and verb are left in (XVII.13). Like Priscian, Hugh further recognized the priority of the subject over the predicate:

Dux quidem verbi nomen est, quia personam significat, quae prior est, cui adiacet actio quae verbo determinatur. (p. 108)

The noun outranks the verb, so to speak, since it signifies an individual, which is prior, and in addition to which there is the action specified by the verb.

Hugh's wording suggests that he viewed *constructio* as a process of adding words to the sentence one by one: first the noun, then the verb, then various modifiers. Evidence that the same idea was in the minds of the Modistae comes from remarks such as the following made by Radulphus Brito:[23]

In constructione relativi cum antecedente ... relativum dependet ad aliquid quod est prius positum in illa constructione, scilicet ad antecedens ... Et dico notanter 'ad aliud quod est prius [positum] in illa constructione,' quia si dicatur 'Socrates videt Platonem qui disputat', cum li 'qui' referat li 'Platonem', tunc li 'Platonem' habet rationem primi constructibilis in tali specie constructionis, scilicet respectu huius quod est 'qui', licet in alia constructione non sit primum constructibile, sed magis hoc quod

In the construction of the relative pronoun with its antecedent, the relative depends on something previously placed in the construction, namely its antecedent. And I make a point of saying 'on something previously placed in the construction,' for in the example 'Socrates sees Plato, who is debating', since 'who' refers to 'Plato', 'Plato' functions as *primum constructibile* in that kind of construction – that is, with respect to 'who' – even though in another construction [i.e., 'sees Plato'] it is not the *primum*;

est 'videt', cuius transitum
terminat. (I.42, p. 244)

rather, the *primum* is 'sees', of
whose change of referent 'Plato' is
the terminus.

The wording 'prius [positum] in illa constructione' is crucial; it supports
Bursill-Hall's suggestion (1966:137) that the *secundum* in each construction is the more optional of the two constructibles, the one that is put in
second in the process of creating the sentence, the one that presupposes the
presence of the other.

All this adds up to a system very much like modern dependency grammar, which treats the head–modifier relation as basic and, like modistic
grammar, often uses the criterion that the dependent element[24] is the one
that presupposes the presence of the other (Vater 1975, Bauer 1979). Such a
criterion is easy enough to apply to endocentric constructions – those in
which the whole construction functions like one of its elements, (for
example, a noun–adjective pair behaves like a noun) – but breaks down in
exocentric constructions, those in which neither part by itself has the
same function as the whole, and hence neither part can be described as
optional. The classic examples are the subject–verb construction and the
preposition–object construction. For ontological reasons the Modistae
have treated the subject as prior to the verb and the prepositional object as
prior to the preposition (which they consider to be a modifier or marker),
while modern dependency grammarians, appealing to morphological government and strict subcategorization as supplementary criteria, have generally treated the verb and the preposition as the heads of the two respective
constructions, though the issue is far from settled (see for example Hudson
1980).

The whole system as presented by Thomas of Erfurt can be summarized
by repeating the lists in (1) and (2) with added superscripts to mark *primum*
([1]) and *secundum* ([2]):

(6)   Intransitive constructions:

   (a)   [1]*Socrates* [2]*legit*   'Socrates reads'

   (b)   [2]*a* [1]*Socrate*   'from Socrates'

   (c)   [1]*Socrates* [2]*albus*   'white Socrates'

   (d)   [1]*currit* [2]*bene*   'runs well'

(e)   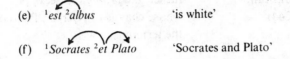¹*est* ²*albus*   'is white'

(f)   ¹*Socrates* ²*et Plato*   'Socrates and Plato'

(7)   Transitive constructions:

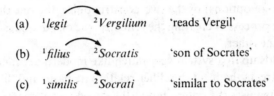

(a)   ¹*legit*   ²*Vergilium*   'reads Vergil'

(b)   ¹*filius*   ²*Socratis*   'son of Socrates'

(c)   ¹*similis*   ²*Socrati*   'similar to Socrates'

(The relations in *Socrates et Plato* are somewhat problematic; see section 5.1 below.)

Combining Thomas's definition of transitivity with the idea that the *primum–secundum* relation represents the order in which the words are introduced into the sentence leads to the intuitively appealing conclusion that to establish a transitive construction is to introduce a new referent. Consider for instance the sentence *Socrates senex videt Platonem iuvenem.* It begins with a simple subject, *Socrates.* To this is added a verb, *videt,* resulting in the structure:

(8)

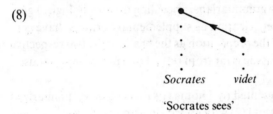

Socrates   videt

'Socrates sees'

(Here I use the same notation as in Chapter 3.) An object is added next:

(9)

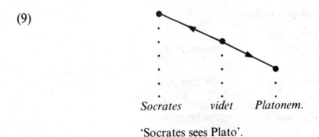

Socrates   videt   Platonem.

'Socrates sees Plato'.

The introduction of this object has brought in a new referent and hence involved the creation of a transitive construction. The two remaining constructions are intransitive, and hence adding the words that they bring in does not introduce any additional referents:

(10)

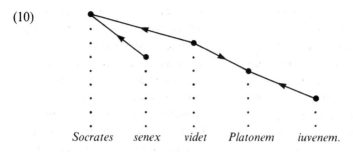

        Socrates   *senex*   *videt*   *Platonem*   *iuvenem.*

        'Old Socrates sees young Plato.'

Hence, far from ignoring the original referential definition of transitivity, the late modistic analysis of Thomas of Erfurt and Radulphus Brito incorporates its fundamental insights in a clear way. The elegance of this analysis served to lock into place all the (hitherto somewhat uncertain) assignments of grammatical relations in the various constructions; the consistency of the whole system became the most important criterion for identifying *primum, secundum, dependens,* and *terminans* in particular cases.

4.6 Grammaticality

The Modistae held that syntax consists of three stages or components (*passiones sermonis,* 'things undergone by speech'): *constructio, congruitas,* and *perfectio. Constructio* is of course syntactic structure itself; *congruitas* is the well-formedness of individual constructions; and *perfectio* is the completeness of the sentence. In this sequence, each *passio* presupposes what precedes it.

    The three *passiones* are implicit in Priscian's definition of the sentence (*oratio* or *constructio*) as 'congrua dictionum ordinatio, sententiam perfectam demonstrans' (II.15), but the idea that they form a linear sequence is distinctively modistic. Neither Petrus Helias nor Magister Jordanus arranges *constructio, congruitas,* and *perfectio* into a series. Pseudo-

Kilwardby notes that *perfectio* presupposes *congruitas*,[25] but the complete ordered set of three does not appear until the time of the Modistae proper:

His habitis dicendum est de quibusdam passionibus grammaticalibus ... et prius de constructione quam de aliis, secundo de congruitate, tertio de perfectione. Et patet ordo, quia perfectio praesupponit congruitatem, congruitas vero constructionem. Omnis enim oratio perfecta est congrua et constructa, sed non convertitur sermo. (Martin of Dacia, p. 87)

Next it is necessary to treat certain things that go on in grammar ... and syntactic structure before the others, then well-formedness, then sentence completeness. The rationale for the order is clear, since completeness presupposes well-formedness and well-formedness presupposes structure. Every complete sentence is well-formed and structured, but the statement cannot be made the other way around.

Since my principal concern in this study is how the Modistae described sentence structure – *constructio* – I shall not explore all the ramifications of the theory of grammaticality (*congruitas* and *perfectio*); to do so would take me far afield. However, it is essential to review the main points. The theory of grammaticality is virtually the same from Martin of Dacia onward; in addition to Martin's exposition, my main sources will be those of Thomas of Erfurt and Radulphus Brito.

If *constructio* is the pairing of words, then *congruitas* is the pairing of their modes of signifying; that is, *congruitas* is a well-formedness condition that applies to every individual construction and requires the modes of signifying of the words thus joined to be compatible. As noted in section 3.2 above, compatibility of modes of signifying is distinct from compatibility of meanings; a semantically anomalous but grammatical phrase like *cappa categorica* has the former but not the latter.

Grammaticality conditions are always stated in terms of requirements imposed on the *terminans* by the *dependens*, apparently because *dependere* had been identified with *regere*, 'to govern', and *exigere*, 'to require'. This leads to occasional odd-sounding statements. For instance, in the noun–adjective construction, the adjective has to agree in gender, number, and case with the noun it modifies; but the adjective, not the noun, is the *dependens* and thus has to be viewed as exerting the requirement. This makes it impossible for the Modistae to say that the noun requires the adjective to agree with it in gender, number, and case; instead they say that the adjective picks up its gender, number, and case from the noun as respective modes of signifying, and that these modes in the adjective, once present, exert a requirement that the corresponding modes of signifying in the noun be the same.

This analysis figures in Thomas of Erfurt's explanation of why grammaticality sometimes requires modes of signifying to match (i.e., display concord) and sometimes requires a different kind of compatibility, in which the modes that are paired with each other are complementary rather than alike:

Tertio notandum est quod . . . duplex est conformitas, scilicet proportionis et similitudinis; et quandoque utraque ad constructionem requiritur, quandoque autem sufficit proportionis tantum, quandoque autem sufficit similitudinis conformitas tantum.

Third, note that there are two kinds of compatibility, namely complementary pairing and matching; sometimes both are required for a construction, while sometimes complementary pairing, and sometimes matching, is sufficient by itself.

Et ut sciamus quando utraque conformitas exigatur . . . est sciendum quod quandoque constructibile dependens habet aliquos modos significandi, non ex proprietatibus suae rei per se, sed ex proprietatibus rei constructibilis terminantis; et tunc inter illos modos significandi exigitur similitudo, et non proportio . . . ut patet de constructione adiectivi cum substantivo et in constructione suppositi nominativi casus cum verbo personali. Nam adiectivum habet tam genus, quam numerum, quam personam ex proprietatibus rei subiectae, ut dictum est supra. Unde ex parte substantivi non requirit modos

And to know which kind of compatibility is required when, one must know that sometimes the *dependens* gets some of its modes of signifying, not from properties of the thing that it itself stands for, but from properties of the thing signified by the *terminans*; and what is required between such modes of signifying is matching, not complementarity . . . as is evident from the noun–adjective construction, and the construction of a nominative subject with a personal verb. For the adjective has gender, number, and person derived from the properties of the thing it is predicated of, as noted above. Hence it requires on the

proportionabiles, sed similes.
Similiter verbum personale habet
numerum, et personam, ex
proprietatibus rei suppositae; ideo
hos modos requirit in supposito,
non proportionabiles, sed similes.

Si autem constructibile dependens
habet aliquos modos significandi
ex proprietatibus suae rei per se, et
non ex proprietatibus rei
constructibilis terminantis, tunc
exigitur in illis modis significandi
proportio, et non similitudo. Et
quia adiectivum habet modum
adiacentis proprie et de
proprietatibus suae rei, ideo ...
requirit in subiecto modum per se
stantis, qui est sibi proportionalis.
(*Grammatica speculativa*, p. 310)

part of the substantive not
complementary modes, but
matching ones. Likewise, the
personal verb receives its number
and person from the properties of
the thing signified by the subject;
hence it requires that these modes
be matched, not just
complemented, in the subject.

If, however, the *dependens* gets
certain modes of signifying from
properties of the thing it signifies
by itself, and not from properties
of the thing signified by the
terminans, then what is required
in these modes of signifying is
complementarity, not matching.
And since the adjective has the
mode that makes it an adjective
in and of itself, on the basis of
properties of what it signifies ...
it requires that the word it
is predicated of have a mode
of signifying that makes it a
noun substantive; the substantive
and adjective modes are
complementary.

The term *proportio*, which I translate as 'complementary pairing', refers to
a relation between two entities in which they are not identical, but nonetheless in some sense belong together. This is the term used to refer to the
relation of proportionateness between cause and effect in Aristotle's
Posterior analytics (I.1–5); it translates Aristotle's term ἀναλογία.[26] The
Modistae sometimes use *proportio* in a broader sense to encompass both
proportio (strict sense) and *similitudo*.

In this context it is helpful to think of modes of signifying as bundles of
features attached to lexical items. The interaction of the modes of signifying in a construction like *Socrates albus* can then be visualized as follows:

(11)

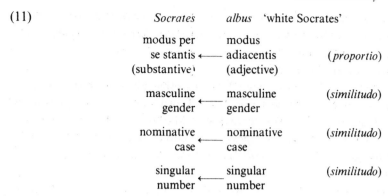

	Socrates	*albus*	'white Socrates'
	modus per se stantis ←	modus adiacentis	(*proportio*)
	(substantive)	(adjective)	
	masculine gender ←	masculine gender	(*similitudo*)
	nominative case ←	nominative case	(*similitudo*)
	singular number ←	singular number	(*similitudo*)

The whole theory can be illustrated more fully by taking another example, one in which Martin of Dacia not only presents an analysis, but argues for it in opposition to an older analysis of the same construction.[27] According to the (presumably pre-modistic) grammarians that Martin is arguing against, the requirements for grammaticality of the subject–verb construction comprise six *accidentia*, three in the noun and three in the verb:

(12)

	Socrates	*currit*	'Socrates runs'
	third person —	third person	
	singular number —	singular number	
	nominative case —	finite mood	

This analysis presupposes some kind of pairing, but is vague as to what kind; the fact that it mentions *accidentia* rather than modes of signifying suggests that it dates from well before the rise of modistic grammar. The requirement that the subject and verb agree in number excludes ungrammatical constructions such as *Socrates currunt*; the rule that they must agree in person excludes *Socrates scribo*; and the rule that the finite verb takes its subject in the nominative excludes *Socratem currit* and the like.

Martin's objection to this analysis is that it does not rule out *albus currit*, 'white runs' (which would be grammatical if another element, such as 'man', were understood, but is not grammatical by itself). The theoretical issue involved is whether the conditions for grammaticality can be stated purely in terms of *accidentia* (i.e., in modistic terms, accidental modes of signifying); Martin takes the ungrammaticality of *albus currit* as evidence that they cannot, since the difference between substantive and adjective, which distinguishes *albus currit* from *Socrates currit*, is an essential rather than accidental mode.

Hence it is necessary to require that the subject be a noun substantive – that is, that it have a *modus per se stantis*. To what mode of signifying on the part of the verb does this correspond? Martin's answer is that it corresponds to what he calls *compositio*, the copula implicit in every verb (as for example 'runs' = 'is running');[28] he does not claim originality on this point.

There is also the question of whether it is correct to say, as for example Pseudo-Kilwardby had done, that the finite mood of the verb corresponds to the nominative case of the subject.[29] The objection is that there are finite verbs that govern cases other than the nominative (such as *taedet*, 'be weary of', in example (5) above, which takes what is semantically its subject in the accusative, and its object in the genitive). Hence Martin reasons that the finite mood of the verb has to correspond, not to the nominative case in particular, but to *casus simpliciter* – case in and of itself, without regard to which case it is – and the fact that the subject of *currit* is in the nominative is accounted for by yet another property of the verb, which Martin calls *modus significandi ut in altero*, 'mode of signifying as on the part of another.' In defense of this proposal he gives an interesting summary of how to argue for modes of signifying:

Et tu dices forte quod fictus est, cum nulli auctorum de ipso unquam fecerunt mentionem. Dico quod ipsum non fingo, sed a re probo.

And you may say that [the *modus ut in altero*] is fictitious, since none of the authorities have ever made any mention of it. I say that I am not making it up, and I shall prove it from the evidence.

Iuxta quod notandum quod tripliciter contingit arguere modos significandi: uno modo a re ipsa quasi a modis essendi, dicendo quod tales sunt modi essendi in re, ergo ipsa res significata per vocem tales debet habere modos significandi, et hic est modus

In this connection, note that there are three ways to argue for modes of signifying; one way is from the thing signified, as from the *modi essendi*, saying that there are such-and-such *modi essendi* in the thing itself, and therefore that the linguistic representation of that

arguendi a causa, et forte non pertinet ad grammaticos, sed magis ad superiorem artificem utpote ad metaphysicum.

thing ought to have particular modes of signifying. This is the method of arguing from causes and is perhaps not applicable to the grammarian, but rather to the practitioner of a higher art, i.e., the metaphysician.

Alius est modus arguendi a constructione, ut dicendo: haec constructio est talis, ergo habet tales modos significandi, et est modus arguendi ab effectu. Et hic modus arguendi est grammatici. Ipse enim grammaticus tam constructionem quam modos significandi per se considerat.

Another way is to argue from syntax, as in saying 'This construction is of such-and-such a type and therefore involves such-and-such modes of signifying;' this is the method of arguing from effects. And this is the grammarian's method of arguing. For the grammarian himself properly considers both construction and mode of signifying.

Tertius est modus arguendi modos significandi in dictionibus ... sicut si per modum dependentis arguatur modus terminantis. Unde si dicatur in aliqua constructione: haec dictio habet modum significandi per modum dependentis, ergo reliqua habet modum terminantis, supposito quod sit constructio inter ipsas. (pp. 99–100)

There is a third way of arguing for modes of signifying in words, as when one argues for the mode of *terminans* from the mode of *dependens*. Hence if it is said that, in any construction, 'This word has the mode of signifying that makes it the *dependens*,' it follows that the other word has the mode of signifying that makes it the *terminans*, given that the two are linked by *constructio*.

The argument for the *modus ut in altero*, then, is simple: there has to be something in the verb that corresponds to the nominative case in the noun, and this is it. Likewise, Martin says that if the noun is genitive, the verb has a *modus ut est alterius*; if dative, a *modus ut ipsum alteri* (p. 100). The complete set of correspondences for the subject–verb construction is then:

(13)

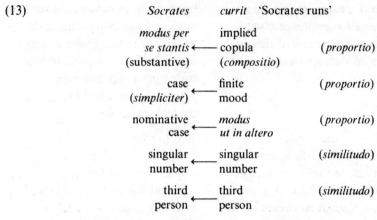

	Socrates	*currit* 'Socrates runs'
modus per se stantis ⟵ (substantive)	implied copula (*compositio*)	(*proportio*)
case (*simpliciter*) ⟵	finite mood	(*proportio*)
nominative case ⟵	*modus ut in altero*	(*proportio*)
singular number ⟵	singular number	(*similitudo*)
third person ⟵	third person	(*similitudo*)

The later Modistae made only minor changes in this analysis, mostly comprising changes of terminology. An indication of the changes that were made can be obtained by comparing Martin's analysis with the much later one given by Radulphus Brito (I.46, p. 258). The main differences are:

(1)   Another pair of proportional modes has been added: the verb's *modus fieri* (the mode that makes it a verb) corresponds to the noun's *modus entis* (the mode that makes it a noun). That is, the subject is required to be a noun and the verb is required to be a verb. Martin's omission of such an important condition is easily explained: he was reworking an analysis based on 'accidents' and assumed that the essences of the parts of speech (noun-ness and verb-ness, respectively) would be taken care of independently.

(2)   *Compositio* is glossed as *modus dependentis ante*, 'mode of taking a subject.'

(3)   The mood of the verb (*modus verbi* – no longer *modus finitus*, apparently because Radulphus had noticed that the new analysis applied equally well to infinitives) now corresponds, not to *casus simpliciter*, but to *ratio principii*, the ability of the noun to be the 'starting point' of the sentence.

(4)   The mode to which the subject's nominative case corresponds is now called *modus dicibilis de alio sub modo* '*ut ipsum.*' Radulphus is evidently trying to make the terminology clearer, though it is not obvious that he has succeeded.

On the whole, only the terminology has been changed, not the basic structure of the analysis or the theoretical claims implicit in it.

Unlike *congruitas*, which applies to individual constructions, the requirement of *perfectio* – completeness – applies to the whole sentence. All grammarians agree that every complete sentence must contain a nominal element and a verbal element; on this point Pseudo-Kilwardby (p. 96), for example, cites Priscian (XVII.12), Aristotle (*De interpretatione* 16 b 7–8), and Petrus Helias (p. 13).

The Modistae refer to the subject and predicate as *suppositum* and *appositum* respectively. The origins of these terms are unclear; the research of de Rijk (1967a, b) and Ebbesen (1981) suggests that there may have been a time when they meant 'topic' and 'comment' (more literally, 'that which is presupposed' and 'that which is put with it'), but this is not the place to delve into their rather complex history. What is clear is that well before the rise of modistic grammar they had come to mean 'subject' and 'predicate' in more or less the modern sense. To quote a twelfth-century logical work:

Et dicitur subiectum in logica id quod dicitur suppositum in grammatica, scilicet quod construitur cum verbo ex parte ante, ex vi personae. Praedicatum est quod in grammatica dicitur appositum. (de Rijk 1967b: 380)	That which is called *suppositum* in grammar is called the subject in logic – namely the thing that is prior to the verb in construction, by virtue of its having a referent. The predicate [in logic] is what in grammar is called the *appositum*.

It took grammarians a bit longer to decide whether the *suppositum* and *appositum* were individual words or whether they were the two pieces into which the sentence was divided by something like an immediate constituent cut. Thurot (1868:218) cites a treatise that favors the constituent-cut approach:

Simplicis orationis duae sunt partes, scilicet suppositum et appositum ... ut [cum dicitur] 'Socrates bene legit', 'Socrates' est suppositum, 'bene legit' est appositum. Verbum tamen substantivum ... est pura copula, ut 'Socrates est albus': 'Socrates' est suppositum, 'albus' est appositum, 'est' est mera copula.	A simple sentence has two parts, a subject and a predicate ... as in 'Socrates reads well': 'Socrates' is the subject and 'reads well' is the predicate. Nonetheless, a copulative verb is [neither subject nor predicate, but] a mere link, as in 'Socrates is white': 'Socrates' is the subject, 'white' is the predicate, and 'is' is merely the link between them.

One factor that may have inclined pre-modistic grammarians toward this view was that terminist logicians analyzed complex propositions in terms of constituent structure; they viewed the *subiectum* and *praedicatum* as the smallest units into which a proposition, simple or complex, could be analyzed, calling them 'terms' because they terminate the analysis of the proposition into smaller and smaller parts.[30] If, then, the grammatical subject and predicate (*suppositum* and *appositum*) are identified with the logical subject and predicate (*subiectum* and *praedicatum*), then the process of arriving at them is much like that of carrying out an immediate constituent analysis (cf. Wells 1947).

However, by modistic times the view had prevailed that the *suppositum* and *appositum* were single words. This is the implicit position of Martin of Dacia, who uses the two terms to refer to constructibles and holds that all constructibles are single words. Thomas of Erfurt is slightly more explicit:

Notandum quod quidquid invenitur in sermone perfecto vel est suppositum, vel appositum, vel aliquid . . . ad aliquod illorum ordinatum, vel est determinatio alicuius horum trium.
(*Grammatica speculativa*, p. 292)

Note that whatever is found in a complete sentence is either the subject, or the predicate, or something depending on one or the other, or a modifier of one of these three.

The point is that modifiers of the subject and predicate are distinct from the subject and predicate themselves.

The presence of subject and predicate is, of course, only one of the conditions for *perfectio*; there are others. Thomas of Erfurt lists three (*Grammatica speculativa*, pp. 286, 314):

(1) The subject and predicate must be linked in a *constructio intransitiva actuum* (a subject–verb construction).
(2) There must be *congruitas* throughout.
(3) There must be no un-terminated dependencies. For example, *si Socrates currit*, 'if Socrates runs', is not a complete sentence because the 'if' implies a dependency on something in another clause.

Radulphus Brito adds a fourth: the predicate has to be a finite verb, not an infinitive, since *Socratem currere*, 'for Socrates to run', is not a sentence (I.75, p. 343). Thomas had handled this as a special case of the requirement that there be no un-terminated dependencies, on the ground that the infinitive necessarily depends on something in the main clause (presumably the verb) and so cannot stand alone.[31]

Of course, the subject and predicate do not always have to be expressed overtly; one or the other of them can be conveyed to the hearer implicitly without being included in the utterance as actually pronounced. The most common case of this is the omission of a definite pronominal subject. Thomas of Erfurt calls this situation *perfectio secundum intellectum* ('completeness by virtue of understanding') and explains:

Perfectio secundum intellectum est, cum constructibilia secundum vocem non experimuntur, sed alterum ab intellectu apprehenditur, ut dicendo 'lego'. Nam hoc verbum 'lego' dat intelligere suppositum, quod est li 'ego', sub conformitate omnium modorum significandi requisitorum ad hanc speciem constructionis. Et tamen hic nulla derelinquitur dependentia ... non terminata, quae retrahat eam ab eius fine, qui est ... perfectum sensum in animo auditoris generare; et ita intelligitur de aliis. (*Grammatica speculativa*, p. 318)	There is completeness by virtue of understanding when constructibles are not expressed vocally, but one of them is understood in the mind of the hearer, as in *lego*, 'I read.' For the verb *lego* implies a subject, which is 'I', with compatibility of all the modes of signifying that are required for this kind of construction. And nonetheless, in this example, no dependency is left un-terminated that would hold the sentence back from its ultimate goal, which is to give rise to a complete thought in the mind of the hearer; and other cases are to be understood the same way.

According to Radulphus Brito, the fact that the understood element is understood to be the grammatically correct one entails that *congruitas secundum intellectum* is also involved.

One point on which all the Modistae agree is that the completeness of the sentence is defined by its ability to carry out its communicative function, which is to express a compound concept and thereby convey a complete thought to the hearer; that is, for them, the concept 'complete sentence' has a functional basis rather than being defined by an arbitrary formation rule like Chomsky's S → NP VP. Thomas of Erfurt, who is most explicit on this point, holds that the function of the sentence is to express a mental concept that is compound *secundum distantiam* – roughly, one in which two simple concepts are joined with the maximum semantic or conceptual distance between them (*Grammatica speculativa*, p. 313). To take an example, *homo albus*, 'white man', expresses a concept that is compound but not *secundum distantiam*. In it, the concepts 'man' and 'white' are linked together, but they are not spread out over the whole conceptual space that a sentence would cover; they are grouped relatively close together as if to serve as part of a more complex structure (such as one of Thomas's favorite example sentences, *homo albus currit bene*). The mind is not satisfied with *homo albus* in isolation, but insists on adding the copula to produce *homo est albus*, 'a man is white', with the right amount of semantic distance. (The notion of semantic distance is related to the physical model of the sentence that I shall discuss in the next section.) The full semantic distance required for a sentence exists only between subject and predicate, and only a verb can serve as predicate, since only the verb signifies *per modum distantis*, 'at maximum semantic distance.' (The difference between the verb and the participle is that although the participle signifies the same thing as the verb, it signifies it *per modum indistantis*, 'at reduced semantic distance.') It follows that in order to be complete, every sentence has to contain a subject–verb construction, a *constructio intransitiva actuum*. All the other constructions are, at least in principle, optional.

All of this, however, raises a problem: it is not uncommon for an ungrammatical sentence to succeed at communicating a complete thought. Does this mean that a sentence can be complete without being grammatical?

The classic cases of ungrammatical but successful sentences are the so-called figures of construction – sentences like *turba ruunt*, 'the crowd are running wild', in which a rule of grammar is broken for rhetorical effect (in this case, the verb is plural but the subject is singular). Perhaps because of their association with other kinds of rhetorical devices, the figures of construction were catalogued and described at length by the didactic grammarians and rhetoricians of the Middle Ages, but more or less neglected by the philosophical grammarians. Taxonomies of them had been inherited from both Donatus (*Ars grammatica* III.5) and Priscian (*Institutiones* XVII.155–68); they comprised not only constructions that are ungrammatical under any reasonable analysis, but also constructions that can be regarded as fully grammatical sentences with repeated material deleted or the like. In the twelfth century Petrus Helias summarized Priscian's taxonomy without adding anything substantial to it:

Est autem figura aliquarum	A figure of construction is the
dictionum in diversis accidentibus	joining of various words with

coniunctio aliqua rationabili de causa, quae fit, quando diversi numeri vel diversa genera inter se construuntur, velut si dicamus 'turba ruunt' ... Ideo autem dictum est 'aliqua rationabili causa' quia, si absque ratione diversi numeri vel diversi casus construuntur inter se, non erit figura, sed vitium.

Sunt autem multae figurae secundum quas fit huiusmodi variatio accidentium. Una illarum appellatur allotheta, et interpretatur variatio, et est genus omnium figurarum aliarum. Allotheta enim est ubi variantur genera vel casus vel numeri vel personae vel quaelibet alia accidentia.

Prolepsis autem interpretatur praesumptio, et est ... quando generaliter aliquid praesumitur, quod postea distribuitur cum subiungitur, ut 'reges venere, Latinus, Turnus, et Aeneas' ...

Syllepsis est diversarum clausularum per idem verbum conglutinata conceptio ut ibi 'hic illius arma, hic currus fuit' ...

Zeugma est diversis clausulis eiusdem verbi adiunctio, ut apud Vergilium, 'Troiugena interpres

mismatched grammatical features with some reasonable justification, which takes place when mismatched numbers or mismatched genders are put into construction together, as when we say 'the crowd are running wild' ... We said 'with some reasonable justification' because if mismatched numbers or cases are put together without justification, what results is not a figure, but a grammatical error.

There are many kinds of figure that allow for this kind of variation of grammatical features. One of them is called *allotheta* [ἀλλοιότης], which means 'variation' and is the genus that includes all the other figures. For *allotheta* occurs whenever genders or cases or numbers or persons or any other features are varied.

Πρόληψις means 'anticipation' and occurs, in general, when something is presupposed that will later be spelled out item by item, as in 'Kings came, Latinus, Turnus, and Aeneas' [cf. *Aeneid* XII.161 ff.]

Σύλληψις is the combination of two clauses stuck together, as it were, with the same verb, as in 'here were her weapons, here her chariot' [*Aeneid* I.16].

Ζεῦγμα is the adjunction of the same verb to several clauses, as in Vergil's 'O Trojan-born

divum, qui tripodas, qui clarios latices, qui numina Phoebi sentis' ...

spokesman for the gods, who knowest the tripods, the Clarian waters, the divine counsels of Phoebus ...' [*Aeneid* III.359–60].

Concidentia, quando diversi numeri et diversi casus et diversae personae vel diversa genera coniunguntur, ut hic 'turba ruunt', vel 'pars in frusta secant' et similia ...

Concidence [συνέμπτωσις] occurs when mismatched numbers, cases, persons, or genders are put together, as in 'the crowd are running wild' [Ovid, *Heroides* XII.143] or 'part [of them] are slicing it into pieces' [*Aeneid* I.212].

Sexta appellatur procidentia, quando casus pro casu vel nominativus pro vocativo ponitur, ut 'hoc regni' pro 'hoc regnum', 'fluvius' pro 'fluvie' ... (Thurot 1868 : 234–5)

The sixth one is called procidence [ἀντίπτωσις], when one case is put in place of another, or the nominative in place of the vocative, as in 'this of-kingdom' for 'this kingdom' or 'river' for 'O river'.

The theoretical problem can be stated as follows: if a figurative construction that lacks *congruitas* nonetheless succeeds in conveying a complete thought, does it follow that it is a complete sentence and thus that a complete sentence does not have to be grammatical? Basic as this problem may seem, it is one in which the Modistae display singularly little interest. Martin of Dacia notes that someone has claimed that figurative constructions provide evidence against the modistic doctrine that *perfectio* presupposes *congruitas*[32] – but, although he rejects the theory in which it is embedded, he never gets around to refuting the claim itself. The other modistic and pre-modistic texts I have examined do not mention the problem at all and in general show little interest in figurative constructions.[33]

The two exceptions known to me are the pre-modistic grammarians Magister Jordanus and Roger Bacon, who confront the problem and propose the same answer; Jordanus deals with it in a one-page *quaestio* (p. 66), while Bacon makes it one of the main themes of his *Summa grammatica*. The solution that they propose is that expressing a complete thought involves two things – a combination of modes of signifying and a combination of meanings – and that a figurative construction succeeds at the second of these but not the first. To quote Jordanus:

Ad hoc dicendum quod duplex est intellectus, primus et secundus. Intellectum primum appello illum quem vox primo praetendit, et hoc est modus significandi vel aggregatum ex modo significandi cum principali significato. Secundum intellectum appello quem vox praetendere potest secundario. Dico ergo quod omnis constructio figurativa simpliciter est incongrua quoad primum intellectum; sed quoad secundum intellectum intentum a proferente est congrua, non simpliciter, sed secundum quid.	The answer is that understanding a sentence involves two aspects, a first and a second. The first understanding is what I call that which the word initially manifests, i.e., the mode of signifying or the aggregate consisting of the mode of signifying together with the meaning on which it is based. The second understanding is what I call that which the word can manifest secondarily. I say therefore that every figurative construction is absolutely ungrammatical with regard to the first understanding; but it is well-formed with respect to the second understanding intended by the speaker – not absolutely, but relatively.

Bacon makes it clear that the 'second understanding' comes from the meanings of the words apart from their modes of signifying,[34] and he goes on to analyze a wide variety of specific figurative constructions. As an example, here is his explanation of Vergil's *Urbem quam statuo vestra est* ('The city which I am founding is yours', in which 'city' appears in the accusative rather than the nominative because it has been attracted to the case of the relative pronoun):

Quod metrum exigat quod nominativus non ponatur ibi patet si diceretur 'urbs quam statui' etc., sed cum metrum non sufficit, immo exigitur fortior ratio, scilicet expressio sententiae, sicut enim tactum est, posuit antecedens sub	That the meter requires that the nominative not appear in that position is obvious if one says *urbs quam statui*, etc., but meter is not enough; a stronger reason is required, namely the expression of the thought, as has already been

eodem casu cum suo relativo ad : mentioned; he put the antecedent
designandum omnino identitatem in the same case as the relative in
rei suppositae per antecedens et order to indicate complete identity
relativum. (p. 38) of the things referred to by the
antecedent and the relative.

He goes on to explain that the noun–adjective construction (which involves case agreement) expresses the most complete unity of the things it
signifies, and that in this case Vergil has assimilated the antecedent–
pronoun construction to it in order to express a similar unity. The important point is that Bacon assumes that if a construction cannot be explained
in terms of the rules of syntax, it has to be explainable in terms of
communicative function – that is, to use modern terminology, pragmatics
takes over where grammar leaves off.

4.7 Excursus: the background of the *motus* model

In two important publications Kelly (1977a, b) has pointed out that terms
such as *motus*, *principium*, and *terminus*, which occur sporadically in
modistic discussions of syntax, can in fact be traced to Aristotle's *Physics*
and to the application of physical concepts to grammatical analysis. To be
specific, the Modistae pictured the sentence as a motion (*motus*) proceeding from subject to verb or object, and they analyzed it in terms of
Aristotle's explication of the concept of motion.

This *motus* model of syntax originated well before the rise of modistic
grammar. Aristotle's *Physics* became available in northern Europe in the
late twelfth century; it was therefore unknown to Petrus Helias, but its
influence is clearly visible in the early- to mid-thirteenth-century grammatical treatises of Magister Jordanus, Pseudo-Kilwardby, Johannes le
Rus, and others. None of the grammatical treatises presently known
contains a systematic exposition of the *motus* model; the details of the
model have to be inferred from references made in passing. In fact, it would
not be too much to say that by the time of the Modistae the *motus* model
had the status of a conceptual explication or even a metaphor rather than a
doctrine; within modistic grammar it underwent no substantive development, and no theoretical claims were derived from it per se. For this reason
I shall not attempt to trace all the references to *motus* in modistic grammar;
it will suffice to give the content of the model as determinable from early
sources.

According to Aristotle, motion is the actualization of potentiality; when not actually moving, the object that moves is capable of motion (*mobilis*) but actually at rest (*in quiete*). The motion itself, like all physical changes, is between two endpoints or poles (*contraria* or *extrema*) which are referred to as *principium* and *terminus* or *terminus a quo* and *terminus ad quem*.[35] Between the two endpoints is a measurable amount of space (*distantia*).[36]

Magister Jordanus identifies *motus* with *transitio personarum* and builds his account of the oblique cases around it. He presents (and then refutes) the following counterfactual arguments that the ablative and the accusative are the only oblique cases with which the verb can be put into construction:[37]

Item genitivus significat rem ut est principium eius quod se habet per modum substantiae, dativus autem ut terminus eius quod se habet per modum substantiae; sed verbum non significat per modum substantiae, sed per modum fieri vel agere, quare genitivus et dativus 〈non〉 construuntur cum verbis.

The genitive signifies a thing as the origin of that which plays the role of substance, and the dative, as the terminus of something that plays the role of substance. But the verb does not signify a thing as a substance, but rather as a process or action, for which reason the genitive and dative are not put into construction with verbs.

Item solus accusativus significat rem ut est terminus actus, et solus ablativus ut est principium eius; sed solum tale quod sic terminat transitionem construitur cum verbo; igitur solus accusativus et ablativus construuntur cum verbis. (p. 42)

Only the accusative signifies a thing as the terminus of an action, and only the ablative signifies it as the origin of one; but only (a noun) that can be an endpoint of the *transitio personarum* in this way is put into construction with the verb; therefore only the accusative and ablative are put into construction with verbs.

The wording 'terminat transitionem' is crucial here. In a sentence such as *Socrates videt Platonem*, the accusative case marks the *terminus* (*ad quem*) of the transfer of action from Socrates to Plato. In a passive (*Plato videtur a Socrate*),[38] the ablative marks the *principium*, the starting point of the action. A genitive can mark the origin (*principium*) of the thing signified by a noun (*filius Socratis*), and a dative the *terminus*, as in *nocumentum tibi*, 'injury to you' (Jordanus' example, p. 43).

The conclusion of this argument is contrary to the facts of Latin grammar, so the argument has to be refuted. Jordanus answers it by positing two kinds of *transitio*, strong and weak (*vehemens* and *non vehemens*). Strong transition goes from nominative to accusative or from ablative to nominative, as in the active and passive examples above. Weak transition is what enables a verb to take the genitive or dative, either because a noun is understood in the meaning of the verb (*misereor tui* = *misericordiam tui habeo*,[39] *noceo tibi* = *nocumentum tibi habeo*, p. 43), or because the meaning of the verb itself provides for both strong and weak transition (*dono tibi librum*, p. 43). The distinction between strong and weak transition turns up in modistic grammar, but in connection with a slightly different issue: some of the Modistae appeal to weak transition to explain, not oblique case forms, but prepositional phrases, on the ground that the preposition provides the extra linking power that the verb by itself is too weak to supply. Martin of Dacia (pp. 17–18) and Radulphus Brito (I.71) accept this analysis; Thomas of Erfurt rejects it (*Grammatica speculativa*, pp. 262–3).

The gloss 'Admirantes', a mid-thirteenth-century commentary on the *Doctrinale* of Alexandre de Villedieu, much of which is quoted by Thurot (1868, under the designation 'R'), gives a similar account of the oblique cases (Thurot 1868: 292) and further explains that the *transitio personarum* in the noun–noun construction *cappa Socratis* entails the presence of an understood verb; on some deeper level the structure of the construction is *cappa ens Socratis* or *cappa quae est Socratis* (p. 275).

Martin of Dacia takes the same approach, expanding it as follows (*Modi significandi* 83–5, pp. 42–3):

I. Principium
  1. Principium of an act   Nominative
  2. Principium of a substance   Genitive

II. Terminus
  1. Terminus of act or substance indifferently
    a. 'To which' (*cui*)   Dative
    b. 'From which' (*a quo*)   Ablative
  2. Terminus of an act only
    a. Terminus of the signified act   Accusative
    b. Terminus of the speech act   Vocative

The system has been given an overall restructuring to bring in the other cases. The most interesting new development, though, is the analysis of the vocative as the terminus of the speech act (*actus exercitus*): in saying *O Socrates*, for example, the speaker carries out the act of calling Socrates, and Socrates is the terminus of this act. (If he said *voco Socratem* he would be signifying that act rather than performing it.) This interpretation of the vocative received general acceptance among the Modistae.[40]

Identifying *motus* with *transitio personarum* was by no means a distinctively modistic move. John of Genoa, a late thirteenth-century didactic grammarian and lexicographer working completely outside the modistic framework, went as far as to identify different kinds of construction with movements of different shapes:[41]

Et scias quod tres species constructionis conveniunt seu respondent tribus motibus in natura. Est enim motus rectus, et isti convenit constructio transitiva. Item est motus circularis, et huic convenit reciproca constructio. Et est motus compositus, et huic motui correspondet vel convenit constructio retransitiva. Intransitiva vero constructio non convenit motui sed quieti.	Note that the three types of construction match or correspond to three kinds of motion in the physical world. For there is linear motion, and to it corresponds the transitive construction. Then there is circular motion, to which corresponds the reciprocal construction. And there is complex motion, and to it corresponds the retransitive construction. The intransitive construction corresponds not to motion but to rest.

A different strand in the development of the *motus* model is represented in the *Priscianus maior* commentary of Pseudo-Kilwardby, who identifies *motus* with the copula that is implicit in every verb. Just as a physical motion bridges the gap between two locations, the copula bridges the gap between two real-world entities, a substance and an attribute; for instance, in *Socrates est albus*, the copula *est* links 'Socrates' with 'white'. *Est* is explicitly a mere copula when it takes an adjective after it, but in other verbs the copula is implicit: 'runs' equals 'is running'. This property of containing an implicit copula is called *compositio* (Aristotle, *De interpretatione* 16 b 25) and is separate from the meaning of the verb proper. Pseudo-Kilwardby explains:

Dicendum est quod principalis significatio verbi non est compositio, sed res verbi quae est extremum compositionis. (p. 130)	The principal meaning of the verb is not the implied copula but rather the verb's own meaning, which is one of the two things connected by the implied copula.

In fact, *est* can be either a copula, as in *Deus est infinitus*, 'God is infinite', or a complete predicate, as in *Deus est*, 'God exists' (or rather 'God is existent'):[42]

Ad ultimum dicendum quod hoc verbum 'est' dupliciter potest accipi: uno modo ratione merae copulae, et sic sine extremis nihil est actu; alio modo ratione extremi et sic est aliquid gratia significati. (p. 139)	Finally, note that the verb *est* can be taken two ways: one way as a mere copula that is not actualized without the two things that it joins; the other way, as one of the things joined [by the implied copula], and thus *est* amounts to something because of its meaning.

This same doctrine turns up in Pseudo-Albertus, who explicitly analyzes *homo est albus* as a motion proceeding from *homo* to *albus* (*Quaestiones* 13, p. 82); but elsewhere he identifies *motus* with *transitio personarum* (*Quaestiones* 18, pp. 126, 132).

Viewing the implied copula as something like a physical movement provides the key to the concept of semantic distance (*distantia*) that, according to the Modistae, exists between the subject and the predicate of every complete sentence. According to Thomas of Erfurt, *homo albus*, 'white man', is not a sentence because, although it consists of a subject and a predicate (of sorts), it lacks semantic distance. Adding a copula increases the semantic distance between 'man' and 'white', yielding the sentence *homo est albus* (*Grammatica speculativa*, p. 313; cf. Radulphus Brito, *Quaestiones* I.8). That is, the copula, like a physical movement, operates across a specific distance.

A third use to which philosophical grammarians put the concept of *motus* was that of an objection-forming strategy. Johannes le Rus, who is in any case not a lineal ancestor of modistic grammar, illustrates this; from his point of view, trying to deduce too much from the proposition that *verbum significat motum* ('the verb signifies motion') is a straightforward way to get a supply of arguments to knock down.

One example of this is his discussion of the relation of the intransitive verb to its complement (e.g., *Socrates* in *ego sum Socrates*). The question is what grammatical feature is the basis of this construction, and he begins by presenting an argument that it is person, just as with the relation of the verb to its subject. For the verb signifies motion, and every motion is defined in terms of two endpoints, its origin (which he equates with its agent) and its termination. Moreover, Aristotle says that a motion is an attribute of what undergoes it (its patient) more than of what brings it about (its agent); hence, Johannes reasons, the movement (the verb) belongs with the substance or person of its endpoint (its complement) at least as much as with that of its origin (its agent), if not more so.[43]

The argument rests on a systematic confusion of agent and patient with origin and endpoint, but instead of unraveling it, Johannes argues that the whole approach is inapplicable:

Ad primum dicendum est autem quod duplex est constructio verbi ex parte post. Uno modo fit constructio quando duae substantiae per modum unius construuntur ad invicem, compositione mediante, et talis constructio intransitiva est. Manet enim ut identitas personarum, ut cum dicitur 'Ego sum Socrates'. Et secundum hunc modum casuale constructibile non est ut recipiens actum verbi. Propter hoc non est obiectio de actione et passione. Alio enim modo construitur cum casuali ex parte post ut recipiente actionem et huius⟨modi⟩ constructio transitiva est. (*Quaestiones* 14, Vatican ms., fol. 95ra)

The answer to the first argument is that there are two ways in which a verb can be construed with something that comes after it. One of them applies when two substances are identified with each other and put into construction with a copula between them; such a construction is intransitive, for there is identity of persons, as in 'I am Socrates'. And in such a case the nominal element in the construction is not the recipient of the action of the verb; for this reason the objection about agent and patient does not apply. For the verb is construed in a different way with something that follows it as the recipient of the action, and such a construction is transitive.

Two chapters earlier Johannes constructs and refutes a different straw-man argument from *motus*: citing Aristotle's observation that motions are counted by counting the number of things that undergo them, the number of times they occur, and the number of states in which they end up (*Physics* V.4, 227 b 21 – 228 a 7), he tries to deduce that since the verb does not inflect for number counted all three ways, it ought not to inflect for number at all.[44] He never uses the *motus* model in formulating his own position, and he seems to be trying to give the impression that it is fundamentally misleading. This may have something to do with the fact that he was active at Paris in the early 1200s, when lecturing on Aristotle's *Physics* was forbidden by the Church.

On the other hand, Johannes' contemporary, Roger Bacon, who pursued a lively interest in physics in spite of ecclesiastical disapproval, used the *motus* model freely. There is a good example of this in the discussion of *urbem quam statuo vestra est* mentioned above. One of the questions raised is why the verb has no nominative subject; under the assumption that every verb signifies a *motus*, the question is why there is no nominative case form signifying the *terminus a quo*. Bacon, who holds that the subject is *urbem* and is in the accusative, cites an argument that although the nominative is the usual case for the *terminus a quo*, it is not the only possible one; just as the road from Thebes to Athens is also the road from Athens to Thebes, the case that normally marks the termination of a movement – the accusative – can just as well mark its origin.[45]

5 *Modistic treatments of particular syntactic problems*

The true test of any linguistic theory is, of course, its actual use in the analysis of language. As the Modistae applied their model of sentence structure to the various sentence-types of Latin, they found, naturally enough, that certain structures posed problems, and they argued for or against modifications in the theoretical framework in much the same manner as their present-day counterparts.

Among the important issues in modistic syntax were constituency versus dependency (an issue raised in the analysis of coordinate structures and embedded sentences), grammatical relations in impersonal clauses, and the relation of anaphoric pronouns to their antecedents. In this chapter I shall present samples of the modistic discussion of these issues, drawn mainly from the work of Radulphus Brito. I make no attempt to trace the complete history of each question, but only to give a sampling of the arguments.

5.1 Conjunctions and constituent structure

One of the basic presuppositions of modistic syntax is that all grammatical relations link individual words, not groups of words. That is, the modistic model is a dependency grammar, not a constituency grammar – and, like all dependency grammars, it has difficulty dealing with coordinating conjunctions.

Consider, for example, the sentence *Socrates et Plato currunt*, 'Socrates and Plato are running': what is its subject? In a constituency grammar, there is no problem; the subject is *Socrates et Plato* (as a whole) and the structure is something like the following:

(1)

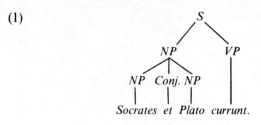

Socrates et Plato currunt.

'Socrates and Plato are running.'

But the modistic model presupposes that the subject relation connects the verb to a particular word. The obvious candidates for subjecthood are therefore *Socrates*, *et*, and *Plato*, corresponding to the following putative structures:

(2) (a)

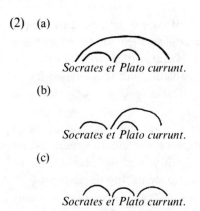

Socrates et Plato currunt.

     (b)

Socrates et Plato currunt.

     (c)

Socrates et Plato currunt.

(I have omitted the arrowheads, which are not relevant at the moment.)

The trouble with calling either *Socrates* or *Plato* the subject is that there is no basis for choosing one rather than the other; apart from minor (and, from the modistic point of view, irrelevant) matters of stylistic effect, 'Socrates and Plato are running' means exactly the same thing as 'Plato and Socrates are running'. Hence neither analysis (a) nor analysis (c) is properly motivated.

As for analysis (b), from the modistic standpoint it would be very odd to claim that the conjunction is the subject of the sentence. After all, a conjunction has no referent and no *modus esse per modum per se stantis*; it has nothing in common with the nouns and pronouns that normally function as subject. A transformational grammarian might get around this by saying that the conjunction acquires the features of the things it conjoins through some kind of feature-copying mechanism, but there was no such thing as feature-copying in modistic grammar; the Modistae held that modes of signifying were more or less inalienable properties of words. (They handled agreement relations by requiring certain modes to be identical in the two words linked, not by copying features from one to the other. In any case, agreement rules involved only accidental modes; any feature-copying mechanism that could allow a conjunction to be the subject of the sentence would effectively be transforming a conjunction into a noun, changing its *modus essentialis generalissimus* and undercutting the whole modistic theory of the defining properties of the parts of speech.)

Such, then, was the dilemma in which the Modistae found themselves with regard to the conjunction: of the three analyses straightforwardly provided for by their framework, two were inadequately motivated, and the third, completely unworkable. It was therefore necessary to change the framework, and one of the more radical changes was proposed by Boethius Dacus, who argued for jettisoning the assumption that the relation between the conjunction and its conjuncts is a syntactic one.

He states his arguments in Question 132 of his *Modi significandi* ('Utrum coniunctio sit constructibilis,' pp. 302–5). The three main points that emerge are the following. First, the conjunction does not require specific modes of signifying on the part of the conjuncts – it can join two of anything, be they nominatives, genitives, accusatives, verbs, prepositions, or adverbs; hence it lacks *principia construendi*.[1] Second, it can join complete sentences (as in 'Socrates runs and Plato debates'), and a relationship between complete sentences which cannot be reduced to a word-to-word linkage is not *constructio*.[2] Third, since the conjunction has no referent, a construction linking it to another word would be neither transitive nor intransitive.[3] On these grounds Boethius concludes that the conjunction does not participate in construction at all. He points out that the conjunction is a syncategorematic term – a word that carries no meaning apart from its effect on the logical structure of the sentence – and argues that this means the relation between the conjunction and its conjuncts is semantic, not syntactic.

Ex officio, quod dictio syncategorematica facit in oratione, intelligi habet suum	The meaning of a syncategorematic term is to be understood from its function in

significatum; namque officium dictionis syncategorematicae est ex suo significato effective. Nihil enim aliud esset significatum huius dictionis 'vel' vel 'si' vel 'an' et harum dictionum 'totus' et 'omnis', nisi haberent diversa officia in oratione sive actiones. Intelligendum etiam, quod officium dictionis syncategorematicae non est ipsum suum significatum, sed est effective ex suo significato. Officium enim huius dictionis 'omnis' est distribuere sive denotare terminum teneri pro omni eo, de quo terminus est dicibilis; hoc enim officium habet in oratione. Hoc tamen non est suum significatum, quia hoc signum 'omnis', existens extra orationem, significat, sed non distribuit, ut de se patet.
(p. 304)

the sentence, for the function of a syncategorematic word effectively arises out of its meaning. For the meanings of these words, 'or' and 'if' and 'whether', or these, 'all of' and 'every', would not differ if they did not have different functions or do different things in the sentence. Understand that the function of a syncategorematic word is not its meaning itself, but effectively arises out of its meaning. For the function of the word 'every' is to distribute, or to show that the term applies to everything to which it can be applied; this is its function in the sentence. But this is not its meaning, for the term 'every', existing outside of a sentence, has meaning, but does not have its distributive function, as is self-evident.

Cum constructio ponitur in oratione est pars illius orationis, in qua ponitur. Sed non construitur cum ea sicut partes declinabiles ... Partes enim declinabiles modos significandi determinatos habent in dictionibus, cum quibus ordinantur in oratione ... Sic autem non requirit modos significandi determinatos coniunctio in illis dictionibus, cum quibus ordinatur in oratione.
(p. 305)

When the conjunction is put in a sentence, it is a part of that sentence [*pars orationis* = 'part of sentence' or 'part of speech'], but is not a part of its syntactic structure in the manner of the declinable parts of speech. For the declinable parts of speech require particular modes of signifying in the words to which they are connected in the sentence. But the conjunction does not require particular modes of signifying in the words to which it is connected in the sentence.

A contemporary logician, William of Sherwood, explains that, from the logician's point of view, the words in a declarative sentence divide up into three classes: the subject and predicate; modifiers, such as 'white', that introduce additional predications; and modifiers, such as 'every', that specify logical relations. This third set, the syncategoremata, includes such things as simple logical connectives ('if ... then', 'and', 'or'), the copula ('is'), negation ('not'), quantifers ('some', 'all'), modal operators ('necessary', 'possible'), and various words signifying combinations of them (e.g., 'no' = 'all ... not').[4] These are the basic building blocks of logical structure. Boethius' claim is that, given that the semantic function of *et* is wholly structural, it does not need an additional, separate syntactic structural function.

This, of course, leaves unanswered the question of what the rest of the structure may be; in particular, does the subject relation connect *currit* to *Socrates*, to *Plato*, or to both? In the text available to us, Boethius gives no indication, nor are other modistic authors explicit on this point. Given what we know about modistic grammar in general, the best guess we can make is that Boethius envisions the verb as connecting to both:

(3)

'Socrates and Plato are running.'

Radulphus Brito at one point mentions a received view that seems to presuppose such an analysis,[5] and it at least avoids the obvious difficulty of having one or the other noun unconnected. Moreover, it results in an analysis strikingly like that of Tesnière (1959: 325 ff.), who likewise holds that both nouns depend directly on the verb and that there is no syntactic dependency relation connecting *et* with its conjuncts. (See also Baum 1976: 102–5 and Matthews 1981: 198–215. For Tesnière, the double-headedness of the phrase *Socrates et Plato* – that is, the fact that its two nouns can have the same grammatical relation to the verb – is called *dédoublement* and results from a transformation-like rule condensing two sentences, *Socrates currit* and *Plato currit*.)

The alternative, mentioned briefly by Martin of Dacia, is to posit that *Socrates et Plato* functions as a single constituent ('unum suppositum quod est primum constructibile,' p. 97):

(4)

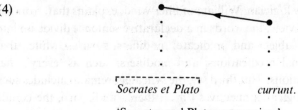

```
Socrates et Plato              currunt.
```
'Socrates and Plato are running.'

As far as I can determine, this proposal is not taken up by Albertus Swebelinus or Simon Dacus Modista in their commentaries on this passage, nor by anyone else. Indeed, it involves such a radical break with the traditional concept of *constructio* that one would expect Martin's mention of it to be accompanied by extensive argumentation, which is not the case. It is possible that Martin was in fact remarking on the general effect of the conjunction, and not the actual syntactic structure that it creates.

In any case, the crucial claim of Boethius' position, as stated, is that there is no *constructio* linking the conjunction with its conjuncts. By broadening the meaning of *constructio* a bit, one can make the almost equivalent claim that the conjunction–conjunct construction, such as it is, is not the same as the other kinds of construction – that, for example, it falls outside the usual division into transitive and intransitive. It is this latter claim that Radulphus Brito, writing some thirty or forty years later, considers and rejects.

Radulphus is defending the proposition that every construction is either transitive or intransitive (I.24); the question is whether *Socrates et Plato* is a counterexample to it. The question to answer, then, is whether *Socrates et Plato* is a construction at all, and Radulphus argues that it is. He cites as evidence the fact that it forms a self-contained syntactic unit ('the conjunction has no need for any constructible other than the conjuncts')[6] and the fact that one can identify the modes of signifying required for the construction (a *modus determinantis et coniungentis* on the part of the conjunction and a *modus determinabilis et coniungibilis* on the part of each conjunct).

This done, he argues that the conjunction–conjunct relation does not stand outside the transitive–intransitive classification – that it is, in fact, intransitive.

Illa constructio est intransitiva, in   The construction in which the
qua posterius constructibile   *secundum* depends on the *primum*

dependet ad prius. Sed constructio coniunctionis cum extremis est huiusmodi, ergo et cetera. Maior patet ex prius dictis. Minor probatur, quia coniunctio dependet ad extrema sicut determinans ad determinabile et coniungens ad coniungibile. Sed determinans praesupponit determinabile et coniungens coniungibile, ergo et cetera. (p. 177)

is intransitive. The construction of the conjunction with its conjuncts is of this type, and the rest of the argument follows. The major premise is evident from points mentioned already. The proof of the minor premise is as follows: the conjunction depends on the conjuncts in the way that a modifier depends on the things it modifies and a link depends on the things it joins. But the modifier presupposes the thing it modifies, and a linkage presupposes the things it joins; the rest of the argument follows from this.

Radulphus bases his argument implicitly on the directions of the *primum–secundum* (or, as he calls it, *prius–posterius*) and referential dependency relations. Since the conjunction has no referent of its own but expresses a relation between the referents of the things it joins, it depends referentially on the conjuncts; further, it presupposes their presence, and hence is *secundum* rather than *primum*. Thus the conjunction falls in a class with other modifiers such as adjectives and prepositions. Every construction in which the *secundum* depends on the *primum* is by definition intransitive, so the conjunction–conjunct construction is intransitive, and the structure of *Socrates et Plato* is:

(5)

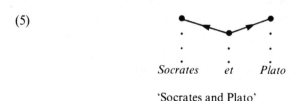

Socrates   et   Plato

'Socrates and Plato'

Another of Radulphus' Questions (I.69) concerns the verb in sentences such as 'Socrates and Plato are running': why is it plural? Note that from the viewpoint of modern theory, this is still an interesting question, comprising two sub-questions: since there is no plural noun in the sentence, where in the overall structure is the plural feature that controls verb agreement located, and how does it get there?

As Radulphus notes, it will not do to say simply that two singulars make one plural. After all, two singulars joined by 'or' make a singular (*Socrates vel Plato currit*, 'Socrates or Plato is running', p. 329). Moreover, two singular verbs do not make a plural verb even if they are joined by 'and'; if they did, a predicate like *currit et disputat*, 'runs and argues', would require a plural subject and would be ungrammatical with the singular subject *Socrates* (p. 328). So the rule that inserts the plural marker, whatever form it may take, will have to apply only to nouns and noun phrases joined by 'and' or one of its synonyms.

Next there is the question of where the plural feature is located. One possibility is that the subject is plural as a whole even though composed of two singular parts; that is, the subject as a whole is a constituent. Radulphus apparently rejects such a constituency approach, though his remarks are brief:

Numerus pluralis non sumitur ex hoc quod habentur diversa, sed ex eo quod aliquid unum significatur per modum unius et indivisi est numeri singularis, et ex eo quod significatur per modum plurificati et divisi est numeri pluralis, sicut 'Socrates' significat aliquid unum per modum indivisi, et ideo est numeri singularis, et 'homines' significat per modum unius plurificati, et ideo est pluralis numeri. Sed dicendo 'Socrates et Plato' non habetur unum per modum plurificati, quia habentur plura. (p. 330)

The plural number does not come from things being taken as distinct, but rather from the fact that whatever is signified as one undivided thing is singular and whatever is signified as multiple and divided is plural. Thus, for example, 'Socrates' signifies one undivided entity, and hence is singular, and 'men' signifies one thing made multiple, and hence is plural. But in saying 'Socrates and Plato' you do not have one entity multiplied, for there is more than one entity involved.

What he is saying is that there is no real plurality in *Socrates et Plato*; if my interpretation is correct, this statement shows that he does not treat *Socrates et Plato* as a constituent (as does Martin), but instead, with Boethius, insists on a pure dependency approach. We can infer that his analysis of the complete sentence would be:

(6)

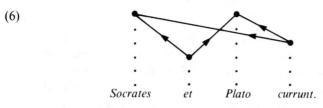

Socrates et Plato currunt.

'Socrates and Plato are running.'

Such a structure leaves no place to put the plural feature.

One could, of course, argue that in such a sentence the normal mechanism of subject–verb agreement does not operate, and that some special rule places a plural feature directly onto any verb that has two subjects conjoined by 'and'. This is a variant of the 'two singulars make one plural' argument already mentioned and is vulnerable to many of the same objections. More importantly, it cannot be formulated as a modistic rule of syntax, since to obey it, the verb would have to 'know' which conjunction was present ('and', not 'or'); that is, the verb would have to exert a grammatical requirement on the conjunction, and this would only be possible if the verb were linked to the conjunction by a *constructio*, which it is not.[7]

In any event, Radulphus' answer to this Question is surprising: he disagrees with the grammatical authorities and agrees with the straw men.

Communiter dicitur quod ista sit congrua 'Socrates et Plato currunt'. Dico tamen quod secundum intentionem Prisciani et Petri Heliae est figurativa et incongrua 'Socrates et Plato currunt', quia sicut vult Petrus Heliae 'synthesis est ponendo singulare pro plurali sicut dicendo "ego et tu legimus" ibi coniunguntur duo singularia respectu huius quod est "legimus" ita quod ibi est conceptio et etiam synthesis.' Ita etiam in proposito dicendo 'Socrates et Plato currunt' licet ibi non sit improportio quoad

It is commonly said that 'Socrates and Plato run' is grammatical. I say, however, that according to the doctrines of Priscian and Petrus Helias it is figurative and ungrammatical, for, as Petrus Helias has it, 'the figure of *synthesis* exists when a singular is put for a plural, as in "you and I read" [1st pers. pl.] – two singulars are joined to the [plural] verb "read", so that there is *conceptio personarum* and also the figure of *synthesis*.' Likewise, in the example 'Socrates and Plato run', although there is no mismatch of

personam sicut est in ista 'ego et tu legimus', tamen quoad numerum est ibi improportio, quia ibi ponitur singulare pro plurali. Sed ratio excusans istam figuram est suppositorum pluralitas, quia ibi sunt plura supposita, ideo ipsa plurificant appositum. Et propter hoc aliqui ponunt istam simpliciter congruam 'Socrates et Plato currunt' . . . Tamen istud non valet, quia ista ratio est ad excusandum figuram tantum . . .

person as in 'you and I read', there is a mismatch of number, since a singular appears in place of a plural. But the reason excusing the figurative construction is the plurality of subjects, for there is more than one subject, and hence they make the predicate plural. And for this reason some say that 'Socrates and Plato run' is grammatical per se, but this does not hold up, since such a reason only excuses a figurative construction [rather than changing it from figurative to fully grammatical].

Unde dico quod ista est incongrua, 'Socrates et Plato currunt', et quod ista est congrua, 'Socrates et Plato currit'. (p. 329)

Hence I say that 'Socrates and Plato run' is ungrammatical and 'Socrates and Plato runs' is grammatical.

That is, Radulphus holds that, from the standpoint of grammar, the verb ought in fact to be singular. His position is that the use of a plural verb in such a sentence is a figure of construction (albeit one so common as to be practically obligatory), not a rule of syntax. He compares it to *conceptio personarum*, the figure of construction in which conjoined subjects of different persons take a verb agreeing with whichever subject is higher on the scale first > second > third, for example:

(7) (a) *Ego et tu legimus.*   'You and I read.'
          1st   2nd 1st   person
          sg.   sg. pl.   number

     (b) *Tu et ille legitis.*   'You and he read.'
          2nd   3rd   2nd   person
          sg.   sg.   pl.   number

(The same hierarchy determines the word order, which is different from English.) Since these are figures of construction rather than *principia congruitatis*, they are open to some variability and to influence from the intended meaning and rhetorical effect.

5.2 Sentence embedding

The preceding section, leading to the conclusion that at least one modistic analysis of conjunctions made no use of the concept of constituency, was pieced together out of the brief remarks of many authors and was necessarily somewhat hypothetical in tone. In this section, which concerns a constituency analysis that received more general acceptance, we are on much solider ground: there are at least two extant Questions that address the constituency–dependency problem directly – one by Anonymus Norimbergensis and one by Radulphus Brito – as well as some brief comments made by Siger de Courtrai. The principle that emerges is that embedded sentences, as well as individual words, are syntactic units; that is, *dictiones* and *orationes*, but nothing else, are constituents.

The Question by Anonymus Norimbergensis, which was pointed out and partly edited by Pinborg (1980b), concerns the ablative absolute, which is an embedded clause that signifies the cause or circumstance of the event referred to by the main clause, for example:

(8) Magistro   legente   pueri   proficiunt.
     master   reading boys progress
     abl.   abl.   nom. 3rd pl.

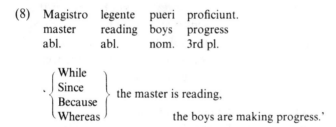

'While / Since / Because / Whereas the master is reading, the boys are making progress.'

The embedded clause has its subject in the ablative (rather than the usual nominative) and has no verb, only a participle, which, agreeing with its subject, is also in the ablative. Any other nouns governed by the participle – objects or complements – appear in the same cases that the verb governs in other constructions.

For the Modistae, the obvious question is whether the ablative absolute is really 'absolute' (ungoverned), as the traditional analysis would have it, or whether it or some part of it is governed by something in the main clause.

Noting that the ablative absolute (or, as he calls it, the 'ablative designating consequence') is essentially a complete sentence, Norimbergensis focuses on the more basic question of whether a sentence can be governed or put into construction. He cites an argument that it cannot, since whatever undergoes construction does so by virtue of its modes of signifying,

and a sentence has no modes of signifying – in fact, if it did, it would be a part of speech.

Regi et construi debetur alicui per modos significandi, sed oratio non habet modos significandi, sed solum dictio; ergo regi vel construi non debetur orationi sed dictioni. Maior patet, quia constructio vel regimen effective derelinquitur ex modis significandi. Minor prout dictionem patet; prout orationem probatur, quia si oratio haberet modos significandi, esset alicuius partis orationis. (fol. 50rb)

A thing obtains the right to be governed and put into construction by virtue of having modes of signifying, but the sentence does not have modes of signifying – only the word does; hence a sentence cannot be governed or put into construction, only a word can. The major premise is obvious, since construction or government is an effect of modes of signifying. The minor premise is obvious as regards the word; as regards the sentence, the proof is that, if the sentence had modes of signifying, it would be some part of speech [or: some part of the sentence, i.e., it would be part of itself].

Another argument is that since a sentence is by definition a free-standing unit containing no un-terminated dependencies, it is impossible for an element of a sentence to govern anything outside that sentence; hence there cannot be a dependency running from the main clause to the subordinate clause:

Item si ablativi in designatione consequentiae positi non ponerentur absolute, sed construerentur cum aliquo et regerentur ab eodem, hoc maxime iudicaretur esse verbum consequentis, sed ab illo non possunt regi, immo nec cum eo construi, ergo et cetera. Maior patet ... Minor probatur, quia

If ablatives designating consequence were not absolute, but were placed in construction with something and governed by it, this would most likely be judged to be the verb of the consequent clause; but they cannot be governed by that verb, nor put into construction with it, and the rest of the argument follows. The

constructibile unius orationis non construitur cum constructibili alterius orationis, neque regit ipsum; sed illi ablativi faciunt unam orationem per se, et ipsum verbum ponitur in altera oratione, ergo et cetera. Maior declaratur, quia constructio vel regimen fit ratione dependentiae, sed constructibile unius orationis non vim habet dependentem ad constructibile alterius orationis, ergo nec ipsum regit nec cum eo construitur ... (fols. 50rb–va)

major premise is obvious. The proof of the minor premise is that a constructible in one sentence is not put into construction with a constructible in another sentence, nor does it govern it; but the ablatives form a sentence by themselves, and the verb is located in the other sentence; the rest of the argument follows. The major premise here is that construction or government takes place by virtue of [referential] dependency, but a constructible in one sentence cannot depend on a constructible in another sentence, and hence does not govern it or go into construction with it.

Item perfecta oratio a nullo regitur, sed tales ablativi in designatione consequentiae positi habent vim perfectae orationis, ergo et cetera. (fol. 50va)

A complete sentence is not governed by anything, and such ablatives designating consequence have the force of a complete sentence; the conclusion follows.

Moreover, if there is a grammatical relation connecting the subordinate clause to something in the main clause, what grammatical relation is it?

Item si ablativi in designatione consequentiae positi cum alio construerentur ut regerentur, hoc esset vel a parte ante vel a parte post; nec sic nec sic, ergo nullo modo. Maior patet de se; minor declaratur, et primo quod non a parte ante, quia secundum Priscianum primo huius, 'omnes obliqui transitivi sunt,' ergo et ablativi, et sic non possunt a parte

If ablatives designating consequence were put in construction in order to be governed [by the main verb], they would be either its subject or its complement; they are neither one, and hence they are not in construction with it at all. The major premise is self-evident; the first argument for the minor premise is that, according to

ante regi vel construi, cum sint transitivi, id est, transitionis termini. Nec a parte post, quia tales ablativi semper antecedunt, quia secundum Priscianum et Petrum Heliam ablativi ad invicem constructi in designatione consequentiae habent rationem antecedentis, ergo et cetera. (fol. 50va).

Priscian at the beginning of the book [XI.12], 'all oblique cases are transitive'; hence ablatives are transitive, and they cannot be governed or put into construction as subjects, since they are transitive, i.e., are the termination of the *transitio personarum*. Nor can they be governed as objects or complements, for such ablatives always precede; according to Priscian and Petrus Helias, ablatives joined to each other to indicate consequence have the function of an antecedent, and the rest of the argument follows.

The subordinate clause is not the subject of the verb (is not construed with it *a parte ante*), since the ablative is an oblique case, and oblique cases mark objects or complements; yet it cannot be an object or complement (*a parte post*) either – or so someone argues – because its normal position in the word order places it before (*ante*) the main verb.[8]

Norimbergensis' position is that the embedded clause forms a constituent and functions as a complement of the main verb.

Dico ergo ad praesens tria: primo, quod huiusmodi ablativi in designatione consequentiae positi, ut 'magistro legente discipuli proficiunt', congrue construuntur cum verbo consequentis a parte post; secundo, quod ab eodem verbo a parte post reguntur; tertio, quod regimen potest ibi ex vi effectus demonstrari.

On this question I have three things to say: first, that such ablatives designating consequence, as in *magistro legente discipuli proficiunt*, form a grammatical construction as complements of the verb of the consequent clause; second, that they are governed by that verb; and third, that the existence of the government relation can be demonstrated from its effects.

Ratio primi est ista: ex ea parte aliqua constructibilis cum alio congrue construitur, ex qua idem respiciunt sub omnibus modis conformibus in illa constructione requisitis. Sed huiusmodi ablativi in designatione consequentiae positi verbum in consequente positum sic respiciunt; ergo et cetera. Maior est evidens; minor declaratur, quia in oratione saepe dicta, 'Magistro' et cetera, hoc verbum 'proficiunt' habet modum dependentis post se sub modo 'ut alio,' nam qui proficiunt alio proficiunt, et istic correspondet in ablativis 'magistro legente' modus terminantis sub modo 'ut quo,' significat enim idem quo proficiunt.

The justification of the first claim is the following: any constructible is construed with any other as subject [*ante*] or as complement [*post*] on the basis of a relation between the two with regard to all the matched modes required in that construction. But these ablatives designating consequence bear such and such a relation [i.e., that of complement] to the main verb; the conclusion follows. The major premise is obvious; the minor premise is that in the oft-used example, *Magistro* ... , the verb *proficiunt* depends on a complement under the mode 'by means of something,' for that which makes progress does so from some cause, and to this in the ablative phrase *magistro legente* corresponds the mode of terminating a dependency under the mode 'by means of which,' for it says by what means they make progress.

Ratio secundi est ista: illud constructibile regit alterum sicut ex ea parte ex qua cogit ipsum stare in tali casu in quo ponitur, ita quod non in alio. Sed verbum consequentis, ut 'proficiunt', cogit ablativos sic poni in ablativo casu quod non in alio, et hoc patet, sic ergo regit eos post se. Maior patet ex definitione ipsius 'regere' ... Minor patet ex dictis: ex quo enim

The justification of the second claim is that one constructible governs another as subject or complement according to the way in which it requires it to be in one case and not in another. But the verb of the consequent clause, *proficiunt*, requires the ablatives to appear in the ablative case and not in any other, and this is evident, and therefore it governs them as

illud verbum habet modum
dependentis post se sub modo 'ut
alio' cui solum proportionatur
ablativus qui est modus 'ut quo,'
exigit seu cogit ipsum antecedens
poni in ablativo ita quod non in
alio, quod respicit in ratione
termini.

complements. The major premise
is evident from the definition of
'govern'; the minor is evident from
what has been said: for in the way
in which the verb requires a
complement under the mode 'by
means of something,' to which
corresponds only the ablative,
which is the mode of 'by means of
which,' the verb requires the
preceding phrase to be put in the
ablative and not in any other case;
it is related to it as to a terminus.

Ratio tertii est illa: ab illo potest
regimen casus in aliqua
constructione denominari, super
quo immediate huiusmodi datur
proprietas a qua sumitur modus
significandi qui est proprietas
ipsius regendi illum casum. Sed hic
proprietas 'ut alio,' a qua sumitur
modus 'a quo' qui est proprietas
ipsius regendi ablativum,
immediate fundatur super
effectum. Videtur enim tale
verbum importare quod efficitur
respectu antecedentis. Sed
effectum immediate consequitur
proprietas 'ut alio' – quod enim
efficitur, alio efficitur – ergo et
cetera. (fol. 50va)

The justification of the third claim
is as follows: In any construction,
the case-government can be given
a name on the basis of that which
has the property from which the
[relevant] mode of signifying is
taken, i.e., the property of
governing that case. But this
property of 'by means of
something,' on which is based the
mode of 'by means of which'
which is the property of governing
the ablative, is immediately based
on its effect. For such a verb
apparently implies that the action
is an effect of the prior clause. But
an effect immediately follows from
the property of 'by means of
something' – that which is an
effect, is an effect of something in
particular – and the rest of the
argument follows.

He holds that if the subordinate clause were ungoverned, there would be no
explanation for its ablative case; after all, a case requirement has to be

exerted by something. As it is, the ablative of the subordinate clause can be treated as a special case of the more general use of the ablative to specify cause or circumstance;[9] the mode of signifying by which the main verb governs such an ablative – the *modus ut alio*, as Norimbergensis calls it – is derived from the real-world property of all actions that they have causes or circumstances. (In fact, the passage quoted is followed, in the manuscript, by a long digression on the relevance of various concepts of causality.)

The structure that Anonymus Norimbergensis proposes can thus be diagrammed as follows:

(9)

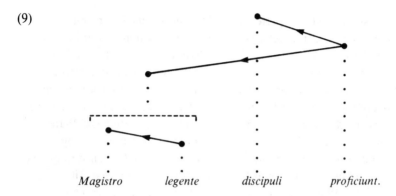

Magistro   legente   discipuli   proficiunt.

'While the master is reading the pupils are making progress.'

His position is that all embedded clauses are constituents – that the clause or sentence per se can have modes of signifying and enter into construction as a unit.

Immo oratio potest habere modos significandi. Et cum probatur quod non, quia si oratio haberet modos significandi esset alicuius partis orationis, nego. Et tu probas, quia 'modus significandi est forma partis dans sibi esse,' et cetera; verum est – modus significandi essentialis sed non accidentalis. Unde quamvis oratio non habeat modos significandi essentiales, potest tamen habere

Contrary to what others say, a sentence can have modes of signifying. And in response to the argument that if a sentence had modes of signifying it would be some particular part of speech, I deny it. And you argue that 'the mode of signifying is the form of the part of speech, making it what it is,' and so forth; that is true – of the essential but not the accidental mode of signifying. Hence,

modos accidentales, ratione quorum cum alio potest construi vel etiam ab ipso regi. (fol. 51ra)

although the sentence does not have essential modes of signifying, it can nevertheless have accidental modes by virtue of which it can be put into construction with another element or even be governed by it.

In support of this position he adduces similar analyses of several other sentence types, of which the simplest is the coordinate sentence:

Certum est quod ista est perfecta, 'Socrates currit', et similiter ista 'Plato disputat', et tamen coniunctio potest inter eas coniungere, immo inter orationes alias quantumcumque perfectas ut 'Socrates currit et Plato disputat', 'sol lucet ergo dies est', 'si pluit, terra madida est'. Ergo adhuc videtur quod talibus orationibus competebat modus significandi ratione cuius poterunt cum coniunctione construi. Alias enim sequeretur quod non esset ibi constructio. (fol. 51ra)

'Socrates runs' is certainly a complete sentence, and likewise 'Plato debates', but nonetheless the conjunction can join them; indeed, it can join other sentences no matter how complete they are, as in 'Socrates runs and Plato debates', 'the sun is shining; therefore, it is day', 'if it rains, the earth is wet'. Hence it still seems that such sentences can have modes of signifying entitling them to be put into construction with the conjunction. Otherwise it would follow that there was no construction in such cases.

That is, the conjunction is linked to each clause as a whole; diagrammatically,

(10)

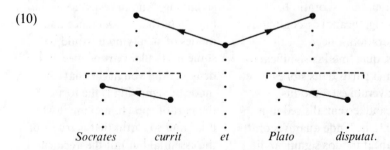

Socrates   currit   et   Plato   disputat.

'Socrates runs and Plato argues.'

This is the same structure as *Socrates et Plato* except that the conjuncts are sentences instead of nouns; Radulphus Brito also discusses it (I.70) and argues at length for the same analysis.

Another is the type of statement in which something is predicated of a whole sentence, as in modal propositions ('X is possible/impossible'):

In propositionibus modalibus dictum supponit verbo personali, ut 'Socratem currere est possibile', verbum autem personale requirit nominativum in supposito, qui in neutra partium dicti videtur esse. (fol. 51ra)

In modal propositions a statement serves as subject of a personal verb, as in 'For Socrates to run is possible'; but the personal verb requires a nominative case on the part of its subject, which does not seem to be present in either part of the statement [that serves as subject].

The point is that since neither *Socratem* nor *currere* is nominative, the (unexpressed) nominative case must belong to the embedded clause as a whole; diagrammatically:

(11)

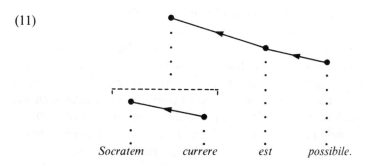

Socratem   currere   est   possibile.

'For Socrates to run is possible.'

Radulphus assigns a similar structure to '*Socrates currit*' *est oratio* ('*Socrates currit* is a sentence', p. 334).

Finally, Anonymus Norimbergensis presents an interesting analysis of sentences with quantified subjects, such as 'every man runs':

Praedicatum enim semper intransitive construitur cum

[In such a sentence] the predicate always forms an intransitive

subiecto et ibi in subiecto signum cum termino communi constituit orationem imperfectam, ut 'omnis homo currit', 'quidam homo currit'. (fol. 51ra)

construction with the subject, and within the subject, the quantifier and the quantified term form an incomplete sentence, as in 'every man runs' or 'some man runs'.

That is, he views quantifiers, not as 'higher predicates' (Carden 1973), but as lower predicates that apply only to the quantified term (compare the passage from William of Sherwood quoted in section 5.1 above):

(12)

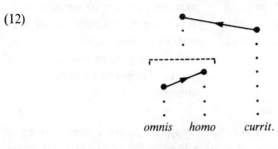

omnis   homo   currit.

'Every man runs.'

The theoretical problem implicit in all these analyses is that of how an embedded sentence can function as a constituent – or, in modistic terms, how a sentence can have modes of signifying and what kinds of modes of signifying it can have. The Modistae seem never to have worked out a full answer to this question. Radulphus (I.70) and Siger (pp. 54, 60–61) agree that the case for a constituency analysis is strongest with structures such as *Socrates currit et Plato disputat* (which is obviously parallel to *Socrates et Plato* and should be analyzed as such), and that in such constructions the only mode of signifying that the embedded sentences need have is an accidental *modus coniungibilis* or the like. Radulphus (pp. 333–4) and Norimbergensis (above) point out that in order to avoid having to conclude that the sentence is a part of speech, one need only deny that it has any essential modes of signifying – accidental modes create no problem. One might have expected the question of how something can have accidental modes while lacking essential modes to turn into a major metatheoretical controversy – after all, things do not ordinarily have accidents without essence[10] – but for some reason it did not; Radulphus and Norimbergensis both content themselves with observing that one can say either that accidental modes do not presuppose essential modes, or that the accidental modes of the whole sentence presuppose only the essential modes of its parts.[11]

In any case, it is not obvious that all of the analyses proposed by Anonymus Norimbergensis can be made to work by giving the embedded sentences only accidental modes. Consider for example *Socratem currere est possibile*, in which the embedded clause is the subject of the main verb. On the standard modistic analysis, every verb requires its subject to be a noun substantive – that is, to have a *modus per se stantis*, which is an essential mode. If the sentential subject has this, it has at least one essential mode of signifying; if it lacks it, it cannot be subject. But neither Radulphus nor Norimbergensis notes this difficulty; in fact, in the analysis of *Socratem currere* just quoted, Norimbergensis bases his implicit argument for the constituency analysis on the fact that the finite verb requires its subject to be in the nominative case (an accidental mode), and hence that if the main verb governed *Socratem* directly, it would be in the nominative and not the accusative (which marks subjects of infinitives).

There remain a few objections to be answered. It was argued earlier that a complete sentence never has any dependencies connecting it with anything outside itself. Norimbergensis points out, however, that the embedded clause *magistro legente* is not quite a complete sentence; it means, not 'the master is reading' but 'while the master is reading', and hence does connect to something outside itself.[12] As for the question of word order (ablative absolute *ante* main clause), he points out that this is no objection to analyzing the ablative absolute as grammatically *a parte post*, since the *a parte ante/post* (*primum–secundum*) relation is distinct from word order.[13] And as for the grammatical authorities who use the term 'ablative absolute', they are speaking pretheoretically ('secundum usum, non secundum artem').[14]

5.3 Impersonal clauses

The analysis of impersonal clauses formed one of the most important proving grounds for the modistic theory of grammatical relations. Many of the Modistae discuss impersonals at some length;[15] in what follows I shall present only the analysis of Radulphus Brito, who covers the field rather thoroughly.

Before dealing with the analysis, though, let us review the data. Most Latin verbs take a subject in the nominative and one or more objects or complements in other cases – most commonly, a direct object in the accusative. In modistic terms, the verb is construed intransitively with its subject *ex parte ante* and transitively with its complements *ex parte post*, as in the structure:

(13)

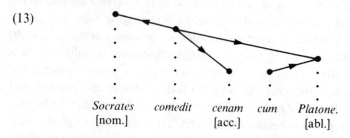

Socrates   comedit   cenam   cum   Platone.
[nom.]   [acc.]   [abl.]

'Socrates is eating dinner with Plato.'

(Recall that the arrows point uphill in intransitive constructions and downhill in transitive constructions.) The verb relates to complements in the same way whether or not they are marked with prepositions; prepositions are viewed as much like extra case markers.

Following what is apparently the standard analysis, Radulphus Brito analyzes the ordinary (personal) passive as fitting straightforwardly into this pattern. He makes it clear that the ablative agent (marked with *a*) is a complement of the verb ('verba passiva construuntur cum ablativo transitive et a parte post,' p. 313). Since all verbs have subjects, it follows that the nominative patient, with which the verb agrees in person and number, is genuinely the subject, and that the structure is as shown:

(14)

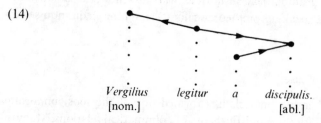

Vergilius   legitur   a   discipulis.
[nom.]   [abl.]

'Vergil is read by the students.'

But Latin also has impersonal verbs. The defining characteristic of an impersonal verb is that it does not agree in person and number with its putative subject, appearing always in the third person singular. A wide range of intransitive verbs form an impersonal with passive morphology:

(15) *lego* 'I read': *legitur* 'one reads, someone reads, reading is going on'
                        (French: *on lit*, Spanish: *se lee*)
      canto 'I sing': *cantatur* 'one sings' (French: *on chante*)
      Quid agitur? Pugnatur. 'What's going on?' 'Fighting.'

Like personal passives, impersonal passives take ablative agents marked
with *a*: *pugnatur ab omnibus*, 'everybody is fighting', *curritur a me*, 'I am
running'. This is a classical construction, discussed by Priscian (see for
example VII.50) and attested in authors such as Caesar and Pliny.

Medieval Latin differs from the classical language in that it also forms
impersonal passives from transitive verbs, which retain their accusative
objects:

(16) *legitur Vergilium*   'one reads Vergil'
      legitur Vergilium ab omnibus 'everyone reads Vergil'

      (cf. the roughly synonymous active *omnes legunt Vergilium* and personal
      passive *Vergilius legitur ab omnibus*)

(On this construction see Thurot 1868:302–4.)

There are also impersonal actives, but, unlike impersonal passives, they
comprise a narrow lexically defined set rather than being formed produc-
tively. There are no more than a couple of dozen at the most; the more
common ones, with their syntactic frames and meanings, are the following:

(17) (a) Verb + genitive (+ circumstantial clause or the like):
           interest mei ut venias 'it is important to me that you come'

      (b) Verb + dative + infinitive:
           licet mihi currere 'I am allowed   to run'
           libet   feel inclined
           placet   like
           vacat   have time
           contingit   happen (to be able)

      (c) Verb + accusative + infinitive:
           iuvat me currere 'I enjoy running'
           oportet   'I ought to run'
           decet   'it is fitting for me to run'

      (d) Verb + accusative + genitive:
           paenitet me huius 'I am sorry for   this'
           pudet   ashamed of
           taedet   tired of
           piget   unable to bear

These are the syntactic frames the medieval grammarians consider cano-
nical, but not necessarily the only ones in which the verbs can occur. In
particular, *placet, iuvat* and a number of others can take personal subjects,
raising the possibility that the infinitives in the examples above should be
analyzed as subjects rather than complements – but Priscian describes all
these verbs as impersonals (XVIII.51), and the medievals appear to have
taken him at his word.

We are now ready to examine Radulphus' analyses. Like Boethius Dacus
before him (*Quaestiones* 90, pp. 209–12), Radulphus accepts the standard
view that although dependency on a subject (*dependentia ad substantiam*) is
essential to all verbs, person is not; it is purely accidental and arbitrary that
Latin has chosen to mark nearly all its verbs with an indication of the
relation of the subject to the speaker. Hence the fact that some verbs lack
this marking raises no particular problem.

Dico quod verbum potest
impersonari, quia persona in verbo
est modus significandi rem verbi
secundum quod est actio
substantiae loquentis de se ut de se
vel ad alium ut ad alium vel de
alio ut de alio, vel persona in
verbo est modus significandi rem
verbi ut est dependens ad
substantiam sub determinato
modo loquendi se habentem ...
Unde licet non potest privari
comparatione ad substantiam
absolute, tamen bene potest
privari comparatione ad
substantiam ut cadit sub
determinato modo loquendi de se
et cetera. (p. 310)

I say that the verb can be deprived
of person, since person in the verb
is a mode of signifying whatever
the verb refers to, indicating
whether it is an act of the speaker
speaking of himself, or to and of
another, or of a third person. That
is, person in the verb is a mode of
signifying that which the verb
signifies as dependent on the
subject from a specific point of
view. Hence although it cannot be
deprived of its relation to the
subject absolutely, the verb can
certainly be deprived of its relation
to a subject having a specific point
of view.

Committed as he is to the idea that all verbs have subjects, Radulphus
cannot analyze impersonal clauses as subjectless. He argues, in fact, that
the subject of the impersonal passive is the agent phrase.

Dicenda sunt tria ... Primo quod
verba impersonalia passivae vocis

Three things are to be said: first,
that impersonal passive verbs take

construuntur cum ablativo a parte ante. Secundo quod talis constructio est intransitiva. Tertio quod est intransitiva non quaecumque sed actuum.

ablative subjects. Second, that such a construction is intransitive. Third, that it is a particular kind of intransitive construction, the *constructio intransitiva actuum* (verb–subject construction).

Primum declaratur sic, quia illud quod habet modum significandi proportionali ablativo potest construi cum eo. Sed verbum impersonale passivae vocis habet modum significandi proportionalem ablativo, ergo et cetera ...

The argument for the first point is that whatever has a mode of signifying proportionate to the ablative can be put into construction with it. The impersonal passive verb has such a mode of signifying; the rest of the argument follows ...

Tertium declaratur, quia illa constructio est intransitiva actuum in qua posterius dependens ad prius significat per modum actus; sed ista constructio est huiusmodi ut de se patet; ergo et cetera. (p. 313)

The argument for the third point is that the *constructio intransitiva actuum* is that in which the *secundum*, depending on the *primum*, signifies *per modum actus* [i.e., is a verb]; this construction is self-evidently of that type, and the rest follows.

Thus the structure of *a me legitur* is:

(18)

A   me   legitur.

'I am reading.'

That this was the standard view is evident from the fact that the arguments he cites against it are weak straw men:

Si construerentur cum ablativo ex parte ante, vel hoc esset transitive vel intransitive. Sed non construuntur transitive, quia vult

If [these verbs] were placed in construction with the ablative as subject, this would be either transitively or intransitively. But

hoc Priscianus quod ablativus construitur cum istis in ratione suppositi, ergo non transitive. Nec etiam intransitive; quia ut dicit Priscianus ista verba impersonalia passivae vocis construuntur cum ablativo more passivorum. Sed verba passiva construuntur cum ablativo transitive ...

they are not put into construction transitively, for Priscian has it that the ablative is put into construction here in the role of subject, and hence not transitively. Nor intransitively, for as Priscian says, these impersonal passive verbs are put into construction with the ablative in the manner of passives. But passive verbs are put into construction with the ablative transitively ...

Item effectus positivus arguit causam positivam. Sed construi cum ablativo est effectus positivus. Ergo debet habere causam positivam. Modo esse impersonale est privativum, ergo impersonale non potest construi cum ablativo.

A positive effect argues for a positive cause. But to be placed in construction with the ablative is a positive effect and ought to have a positive cause. However, to be impersonal is a negative (privative) quality [and not a positive cause], hence the impersonal cannot be put into construction with the ablative.

Item male dicitur 'a me lego' vel 'a me legis' ergo male dicitur 'a me legitur'. Antecedens apparet; probatio consequentiae [est] quia 'lego' et 'legitur' idem significatum habent et eosdem modos significandi nisi quod unum est personale, alterum est impersonale. (pp. 312–3)

'I read by me' and 'you read by me' are ungrammatical; hence so is 'it is read by me'. The premise is self-evident; the proof of the conclusion is that 'I read' and 'is read' have the same meaning and modes of signifying except that one of them is personal and the other impersonal.

Of these, one is an obvious misreading of Priscian (whose *more passivorum* was never meant to establish a point about transitivity), one an inapplicable metaphysical point, and one a confused misapplication of modistic principles. None of them reflects any live controversy.

The case of impersonal passives with accusative objects is more interesting, since such constructions are entirely postclassical and are therefore not sanctioned (or even mentioned) by Priscian. There is a construction in classical Latin that looks superficially similar, in that a few verbs occur sometimes as normal actives and sometimes as deponents (forms that are morphologically passive but syntactically and semantically active – a survival of the old Indo-European middle voice). The standard example is *criminari*, 'accuse (of a crime, in court)': *criminatur te* means 'he accuses you' (deponent form, syntactically active, with accusative object), while *criminatur a te* means 'he is accused by you' (passive of the regular active form). These look rather like *legitur Vergilium* and *legitur a me*. The catch is that since *criminari* is always either clearly active or clearly deponent, it never takes an accusative object and an ablative agent phrase at the same time; it provides nothing to compare to *legitur Vergilium a te*.

It is with such an analogy in mind that Radulphus asks 'whether impersonal passives formed from active verbs take accusative objects, as in *legitur Vergilium*, including with this the question of whether they are construed with the accusative and the ablative at the same time, without using the same word twice' (I.65).[16] Naturally, the real question is not whether the construction exists in the language – of course it does – but rather whether its existence is consistent with modistic theory, and hence whether the theory is observationally adequate. Radulphus argues that the answer is yes, and that the structure of such a clause is:

(19)

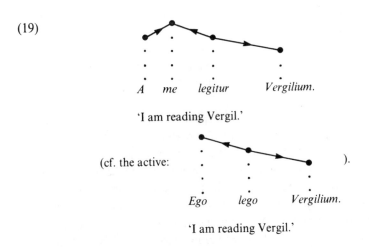

'I am reading Vergil.'

(cf. the active:).

'I am reading Vergil.'

He points out that since the process of forming an impersonal passive from an active verb does not affect the verb's meaning, there is no reason to expect it to render the verb unable to take an object – the crucial point, which he leaves unstated, being that the impersonal passive is not, semantically, a passive.

Illud quod significat per modum transeuntis in alterum ut obiectum vel subiectum congrue construitur cum accusativo qui significat in ratione termini transitus. Sed verba impersonalia passivae vocis descendendia a verbis activis significant per modum transeuntis in alterum sicut verba activa a quibus descendunt; ideo et cetera ... Minor apparet, quia in verbo impersonali passivae vocis descendente a verbo activo non privatur causa qua illud verbum activum a quo descendit construebatur cum accusativo a parte post, sed solum privatur persona quae est in verbo ex comparatione ad substantiam a parte ante. Manente ergo eadem causa manet idem effectus. (p. 316)

That which signifies by means of a *transitio personarum* toward another, such as the one being acted upon or acting, is grammatically construed with an accusative that serves as the terminus of the transition. But impersonal passive verbs formed from actives signify by means of a *transitio personarum* toward another, just as do the active verbs from which they are formed; the conclusion follows ... The minor premise is evident, since in the impersonal passive verb formed from an active, the cause that enabled the active verb from which it is formed to take an accusative object is not absent; only the person-marking relating it to its subject is missing. And if the cause remains the same, so does the effect.

The analogy to *criminari* does not apply because with *legitur*, unlike *criminatur*, the agent and object slots are present at the same time, rather than being alternatives resulting from ambiguity (p. 318).

Finally, there are impersonal actives. In examining whether impersonal actives are possible (i.e., whether their existence poses a problem for modistic theory [I.66]), he returns to the point already made in I.63, namely that person-marking is a pragmatic factor (a matter of the speaker's point of view, *determinatus modus loquendi*) quite inessential to the verb's meaning. In fact, he points out that since the thing signified by the verb can be conceived of without reference to person, and since language can express anything the mind can conceive, it is not merely possible but indeed *necessary* that a language should provide for impersonal verbs to express such personless concepts.

This, at least, is the interpretation arrived at by making a different set of textual emendations than Enders and Pinborg have done. The text as they have printed it says something more surprising – that impersonal verbs 'signify the disposition or capability of something toward an action without dependency on anything in the role of subject, with speaker's point of view unspecified' ('significant . . dispositionem vel habilitatem alicuius ad actum sine dependentia ad aliud ex parte ante sub modo loquendi indeterminato'), which entails that impersonal actives are subjectless and flatly contradicts Radulphus' oft-repeated doctrine that all verbs have subjects.

The text as I wish to read it, corresponding to the second paragraph of Enders and Pinborg's page 319, is as follows:

1 Secundum declaratur, quia si supponamus quod quidquid est possibile mente concipi habet per vocem exprimi et significari,
5 necesse est nos habere ista verba impersonalia activae vocis, quia contingit mente concipere aliqua quae significant in ratione fieri dispositionem vel habitudinem
10 alicuius ad actum sine dependentia ad aliud ex parte ante sub modo loquendi determinato. Adhuc ergo si illud contingit intelligi, contingit per vocem exprimi et significari.
15 Sed hoc modo ad significandum sunt inventa illa impersonalia activae vocis quia significant dispositionem sive habitudinem alicuius ad agere, sicut sunt
20 'placet', 'vacat', 'licet', 'iuvat', et consimilia. Ista enim significant dispositionem alicuius ad agere sub modo fieri sine dependentia ad aliud ex parte ante sub

The argument for the second point is as follows: If we suppose that whatever can be conceived of in the mind has to be expressible and signifiable in language, it is necessary that we have these active impersonal verbs, since the mind is quite capable of conceiving of things that, functioning as verbs, signify the disposition or relation of something to an action without depending on a subject that involves a specific point of view. And since this is capable of being conceived of, it has to be expressible and signifiable in language. But impersonal verbs of active voice were invented for precisely this, since they signify the disposition or relation of something to an action, like *placet*, *vacat*, *licet*, *iuvat*, and the like. For these signify the disposition or relation of something to an action,

25 determinato modo loquendi. Talia
ergo verba sunt sine persona.
Apparet ergo quod possibilia sunt
ista verba impersonalia activae
vocis et propter quid ea sint
30 huiusmodi, quia ut significant
dispositionem sive habitudinem
alicuius ad agere sub modo fieri
sine dependentia ad aliud ex parte
ante sub determinato modo
35 loquendi.

functioning as verbs, without
dependency on a subject involving
a specific point of view. Hence
such verbs are devoid of person. It
is therefore evident that these
impersonal verbs of active voice
are possible; it is also apparent
why they are as they are, since
they signify the disposition or
relation of something to an action,
functioning as verbs, without
dependency on a subject involving
a specific point of view.

The crucial phrase occurs three times, in the lines I have numbered 8–12, 21–5, and 30–5; Enders and Pinborg have made the wording of the three occurrences uniform, but their manuscripts show considerable variation. Both manuscripts have *cum* in the first occurrence of the phrase; the editors' emendation of this to *sine* is, I think, indisputable. *Habilitatem* occurs three times in the paragraph, and in two of these instances one of the manuscripts has *habitudinem*, which is the reading I prefer in all three cases; the two words could well have been abbreviated identically in medieval manuscripts, and the latter reading makes more sense. Finally and most importantly, in the third occurrence of the crucial phrase, both manuscripts have *determinato* instead of *indeterminato*.

As if to confirm this reading, Radulphus leads into the discussion of the next question with a resounding restatement of the doctrine that 'all verbs require subjects, the reason for this being that the relation of verb to subject is the same as that of an attribute to the thing it is an attribute of. But every attribute presupposes the thing in which it inheres, and therefore every verb presupposes a subject' (I.67).[17] He explains that not all verbs require the same kind of subject. The personal active or passive takes a nominative (*Socrates legit*, *Vergilius legitur*), the impersonal passive takes an ablative (*a Socrate legitur*), and impersonal actives take the other oblique cases, genitive, dative, and accusative (*Socratis interest*, *Socrati accidit*, *Socratem taedet*).

If an impersonal verb takes two obliques, as in *paenitet me* (acc.) *huius* (gen.) 'I am sorry for this', which is the subject and which the object? There are three possibilities: either the subject is *me*, or the subject is *huius*, or there is an understood subject ('sorrow') so that both of the obliques are objects or complements.

Radulphus rejects the understood-subject hypothesis on the ground that every verb signifies some real-world entity in the way in which 'be sorry' signifies 'sorrow'; he holds that if we were to posit an understood subject for 'be sorry', there would be no principled reason not to do so for all verbs, impersonal or personal.[18] He apparently does not consider the presence or absence of person-marking to be a sufficient criterion of whether the subject is expressed or understood; but he does not elaborate on this point.

The choice, then, is between *huius* and *me*. Radulphus argues that *me* is the subject on semantic grounds (in this construction 'the accusative seems to bear its meaning in the role of the origin of the action, and the genitive, more in the role of its endpoint'[19]), leading to the structure:

(20)

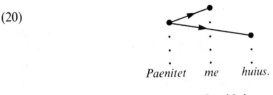

Paenitet   me   *huius.*

'I am sorry for this.'

with the same subject as its English or French translation.

At this point Radulphus would seem to be treading on uncertain ground – perhaps influenced a bit too much by the vernacular language – except that he backs up his analysis with a solid piece of syntactic evidence. He notes that the corresponding participial construction is *paenitens huius*, with the genitive still in place but the accusative gone (its semantic role being taken over by the noun that the participle modifies) – and since participles formed from transitive verbs normally keep their objects but lose their subjects, this constitutes evidence that *huius* is the object and *me* is the subject.[20]

5.4 Pronominal reference

Following Priscian (XII.3–4), the Latin grammarians divide pronouns into two classes, anaphoric and deictic. Deictic pronouns (*demonstrativa*) are those that the speaker uses to point out objects in his environment ('this', 'that'); anaphors (*relativa*) are those that refer to entities already mentioned, comprising what are today called anaphoric pronouns ('he', 'she', 'it') and also relative pronouns ('who', 'which'), as in the example:

(21)   *This* is a book *which* I have bought. *It* cost twenty dollars.

Modern
terms: Deictic   Relative   Anaphoric

Medieval
terms: *Demons-*   *Relativum*   *Relativum*
              trativum

(Our terms 'deictic' and 'anaphoric' are from Apollonius' Περὶ ἀντωνυμίας; the relevant passage is on pp. 5–6 of volume 1 of Schneider's edition of his works.)

For the medievals, the main theoretical problem connected with anaphora was the nature of co-reference (*relatio*). This was a particular concern of the terminist logicians who preceded the rise of the Modistae, and their conclusions were taken up into contemporary grammatical treatises, though interest in co-reference waned during the modistic period and was not taken up again in the revival of terminism associated with Ockham.

The terminists distinguished many types and subtypes of reference (*suppositio*). One of the most important distinctions was between *suppositio personalis*, in which a word stands for one or more of the real-world individuals to which it is applicable (e.g., 'man' in 'a man is running', 'some man is running', 'all men are running'), and *suppositio simplex*, in which it stands not for the individuals, but for the whole concept or metaphysical universal that it signifies ('man is a species', 'man is the noblest of creatures').[21] In a similar way the terminists distinguished two kinds of anaphoric co-reference, *relatio personalis* and *relatio simplex*, depending on whether the anaphor and its antecedent are united at the level of real-world individuals or at the level of metaphysical or conceptual universals.[22]

In ordinary anaphora, the pronoun and antecedent meet at the level of individuals, thus:

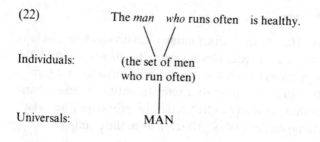

(22)   The *man* *who* runs often   is healthy.

Individuals: (the set of men
                    who run often)

Universals: MAN

Here 'man' and 'who' refer to the same set of individual men; this is *relatio personalis*. There are, however, sentences in which the antecedent and anaphor meet only at the level of universals, in what is called *relatio simplex*. This is of course what happens if the anaphor and antecedent are both in *suppositio simplex* and thus refer only to universals in the first place:

(23)   *Man, who* alone has the use of reason, is the noblest of creatures.

Individuals: — — — — — (no referent at this level)

Universals: MAN

However, *relatio simplex* can also come about when the antecedent and anaphor are in *suppositio personalis* but have different referents, as in the classic example *Mulier quae damnavit salvavit*:

(24)   *Woman,   who* brought condemnation, also brought salvation.

Individuals: Eve   Mary

Universals: WOMAN

(There are of course various other cases, such as one *suppositio simplex* paired with one *suppositio personalis*, and various use–mention mixtures such as 'This man is Socrates, which is a proper noun'. The tendency was to classify every *relatio* that was not clearly *personalis* as *simplex*.)

Unlike *suppositio*, *relatio* became part of the subject matter of grammatical, as well as logical, treatises in the twelfth and thirteenth centuries, presumably because of its connection with the classification of pronouns. Alexander de Villa Dei mentions it in the *Doctrinale*, and there are extensive discussions of it in the grammars of Robert Blund (c. 1175–1200) and Sponcius Provincialis (1242).[23]

All of this was in the background by the time of Radulphus Brito; that is, it was part of the body of elementary knowledge that practically all logicians and grammarians were familiar with, but which no longer represented a topic of active investigation. In any case, the distinction between logic and grammar had grown sharper, and *relatio* was no longer treated under grammar. The issue for Radulphus was a purely syntactic one: is there a *constructio* connecting the anaphor to its antecedent? Petrus Helias had said that there is not; the anaphor *refertur ad* its antecedent but *construitur cum* elements of its own clause only (pp. 49–50).

Radulphus considers the case for this position carefully (I.42, 'Utrum relativum construatur cum suo antecedente'). The heart of the argument for it is that there is no reason to posit a *constructio* of anaphor with antecedent because neither of them exerts any grammatical requirements on the other. There are examples of mismatch in case, gender, person, and number:[24]

(25)

Case:	*Socrates* currit *quem* video.
	[nom.] [acc.]
	'Socrates, whom I see, is running.'
Gender:	ex *semine* tuo *qui* est Christus
	[neut.] [masc.]
	'from Thy seed, which is Christ'
Person:	*ego* sum *qui* [ego] sum
	[1st] [3rd]
	'I am who I am'
Number:	Deus creavit *hominem*; masculum et feminam creavit *eos*.
	[sg.] [pl.]
	'God created man; male and female He created them.'

But Radulphus does not consider the evidence conclusive. He replies that, on the contrary, the anaphor does exert at least one grammatical requirement, in that it requires its antecedent to be a substantive, rather than an adjective; hence the anaphor and antecedent are linked by a *constructio* across which the requirement operates. The anaphor is *dependens*, since it depends on the antecedent for its referent, and the antecedent is *primum*, since its presence is presupposed.

Dico ad quaestionem tria: primo quod relativum habet construi	In response to the question I say three things: first, that the anaphor

cum suo antecedente; secundo quod illa constructio est intransitiva; tertio quod est intransitiva non quaecumque, sed determinabilis cum determinatione.

Primum probatur quia constructibilia quae secundum modos significandi conformes uniuntur, ipsa ad invicem construuntur. Sed relativum et antecedens sunt huiusmodi, ergo etc ... Minor declaratur, quia relativum de suo modo significandi significat per modum dependentis referentis rem antelatam in comparatione ad actum. Sed antecedens significat per modum terminantis dependentiam sub modo referibilis. Sed modus dependentis referentis et modus terminantis dependentiam referibilis ad invicem proportionantur; ergo et cetera.

Secundum probatur, quia illa constructio est intransitiva ut prius apparuit in qua postremum constructibile dependet ad aliud quod est primum constructibile in tali constructione. Sed sic est in constructione relativi cum antecedente quod relativum dependet ad aliquid quod est prius positum in illa constructione,

forms a construction with its antecedent; second, that that construction is intransitive; third, that it is a particular kind of intransitive construction, that of modifier with modified.

The proof of the first claim is that elements that are joined on the basis of compatible modes of signifying form a construction; the anaphor and its antecedent are related in this way, and the conclusion follows ... The evidence for the minor premise is that the anaphor signifies as depending for its reference on a thing previously mentioned in connection with [some other] verb, while the antecedent signifies as capable of fulfilling the dependency and being referred to. But the mode of depending on something else for reference and the mode of fulfilling the dependency and being referred to are complementary modes; the conclusion follows.

The proof of the second point is that, as has already been shown, an intransitive construction is one in which the *secundum* depends on something which is the *primum constructibile* in that construction. But it is thus in the construction of anaphor with antecedent, since the anaphor depends on something previously placed in the

scilicet ad antecedens, ergo et cetera. Et dico notanter 'ad aliud quod est prius [positum] in illa constructione,' quia si dicatur 'Socrates videt Platonem qui disputat', cum li 'qui' referat li 'Platonem', tunc li 'Platonem' habet rationem primi constructibilis in tali specie constructionis, scilicet respectu huius quod est 'qui', licet in alia constructione non sit primum constructibile, sed magis hoc quod est 'videt', cuius transitum terminat.[25]

construction, namely its antecedent; the conclusion follows. And I make a point of saying 'on something previously placed in the construction,' for in the example 'Socrates sees Plato, who is debating', since 'who' refers to 'Plato', 'Plato' functions as *primum constructibile* in that kind of construction – that is, with respect to 'who' – even though in another construction [i.e., 'sees Plato'] it is not the *primum*; rather, the *primum* is 'sees', of whose change of referent 'Plato' is the terminus.

Tertium probatur, quia illa constructio dicitur determinabilis cum determinatione in qua posterius habens modum adiacentis et determinantis dependet ad prius habens modum terminantis determinabilis. Sed constructio relativi cum antecedente est huiusmodi; ergo et cetera. (p. 244)

The proof of the third point is that a construction of modifier with modified is one in which the *secundum*, functioning as an adjective [i.e., crucially lacking a referent] depends referentially on a *primum* that satisfies the referential dependency and is modified. The construction of anaphor with antecedent is of this type, and the conclusion follows.

This leads to structural analyses like the following:

(26)

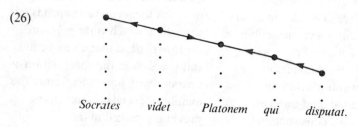

Socrates   videt   Platonem   qui   disputat.

'Socrates sees Plato, who is arguing.'

(27)

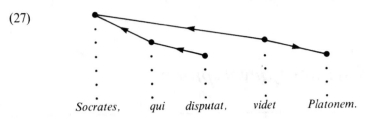

Socrates, qui disputat, videt Platonem.

'Socrates, who is arguing, sees Plato.'

In fact, although he admits that the anaphor and antecedent do not agree in case or person, he holds that they do show concord in gender and number, and that the examples of gender and number mismatch quoted above are figurative (pp. 246–7). He is a little uncertain as to whether this concord is purely grammatical or is a result of the fact that the antecedent and anaphor stand for the same real-world object ('genus et numerus magis consequitur rem absolute,' p. 246).

6 Subsequent developments

With Radulphus Brito and his contemporaries, modistic grammar had reached its apogee, and shortly afterward, metatheoretical objections brought its development to a halt. The objections came from Latin Averroists, such as Johannes Aurifaber (a follower of John of Jandun), and from nominalists such as Ockham. The Modistae, as moderate realists, had assumed that reality had a definite structure that was mirrored in cognition and in language; the objectors challenged this assumption, arguing that words were purely arbitrary representations of thoughts, and hence that the modistic theory of the cognitive and ontological basis of language was untenable.

6.1 The fall of modism

The debate over objections to modism seems to have broken out first, not at Paris, but at Erfurt, which by the early 1300s was the site of an intellectually active group of schools, even if not yet a university.[1] Our first record of it comes from a public discussion presided over by Johannes Aurifaber in October of 1333 (or possibly 1332); an anonymous but detailed report survives and has been edited by Pinborg (1967:215–32). The nominal topic of the discussion is whether *nominativo hic magister* ('in the nominative *hic magister*')[2] is a sentence. Aurifaber quickly gives the standard answer that it is if one supplies a verb – *nominativo 'hic magister' ponitur* or the like – and moves on 'omissis aliis' to the rather different issue of whether there are such things as modes of signifying. He explains his purpose as follows:

Circa istam quaestionem ad alleviandum onus grammaticorum, cum multi sint grammatici per inventionem modorum significandi necnon	Concerning this question, to relieve the burden on grammarians, in view of the fact that there are many who practice grammar by inventing modes of

cotidie generantur, supposita
sincera informatione et sincera
correctione non tamen odiosa, sic
procedam: primo probo quod
modi significandi non sint
possibiles; secundo, quod modus
ponendi et affirmandi eos est
inconveniens; tertio, movebo
dubia et solvam cum ratione
principali. (Pinborg 1967:215–16)

signifying, and such people are
continuing to spring up every day,
and in a spirit of honestly offered
help and correction not meant to
be irksome, I shall proceed thus:
first I prove that modes of
signifying cannot exist, and
second, that the standard method
for positing and confirming them
is unworkable; third, I shall
remove various reasons for
doubting and resolve them with
my basic premise.

Aurifaber's six arguments are, in brief, the following:

(1) Everything that exists is either a substance, or an accident inhering in some substance. Modes of signifying are obviously not a substance; if they are an accident, what is the substance that they inhere in? Apparently the meaning-bearing sound (*vox significativa*), which is what they are said to be properties of; but this cannot be, since *vox significativa* is itself not a substance (it is rather a conventional relation of sound to meaning), and *vox* and *significatio* by themselves, though perhaps substances, do not have modes of signifying. Hence modes of signifying do not exist.
(2) Modes of signifying are supposed to be the causal explanation of grammaticality (*congruitas* and *perfectio*). But there are grammarians, such as Donatus, Priscian, and the non-modistic medievals, who have managed to account for grammaticality quite adequately without positing modes of signifying; hence modes of signifying are unnecessary.
(3) If linguistic signs are arbitrary, then so are modes of signifying – and things that are arbitrary are not a proper object for scientific study.
(4) If modes of signifying existed, their presence would have a visible effect on the form of the word to which they belonged – and no such effect is observed.
(5) It is not necessary to posit modes of signifying in order to distinguish the parts of speech; logicians distinguish nouns, verbs, and syncategoremata on the basis of meaning alone.

(6) Whereas words are arbitrary signs of concepts, concepts are natural
signs of real-world objects (just as smoke is a natural sign of fire). And
if there is nothing arbitrary about conceptualization, it makes no
sense to posit a variety of *modi intelligendi* ('ways of conceptualizing');
the whole modistic metatheory breaks down. (This is the most nominalistic of Aurifaber's arguments; compare Ockham, *Summa logicae*
I.1, and see Andrés 1969.)

In stating his own position, Aurifaber pursues the notion that mental
language is crucially different from vocal language, and that only mental
language is of scientific interest:[3]

Duplex est signum, scilicet quod
per naturam est signum, et quod
per nostram voluntatem est
signum ... Primum signum est
idem apud omnes, et hoc est
conceptus primario rei sive
similitudo in anima ... Sed
secundum signum est vox, quae de
se est libera et per usum nostrum
pro alio ipsius efficitur coarctata,
sine eo, quod sibi aliquid
imprimatur. Ista distinctio patet
principio *Peri hermeneias.*

There are two kinds of sign, that
which is a sign by nature and that
which is a sign by our choice. The
first kind of sign is the same for all
people, and it is the primary
concept or representation of a
thing in the mind. The second kind
of sign is the spoken word, which
is intrinsically unrestricted and
comes to be attached to something
through our use of it, without
having anything additional [such
as a mode of signifying] impressed
upon it. This distinction is clear in
the first chapter of Aristotle's *De
interpretatione* [16 a 3–4].

Grammatica non est de vocibus,
nisi ut de signa habilia et
expressiva conceptuum tam
simplicitum quam compositorum,
et ideo secundum distinctionem
rerum et conceptuum, ut sunt
expressibilia et significabilia per
voces, distinguuntur voces in omni
lingua. (Pinborg 1967:226)

Grammar is not about words,
except insofar as they are adequate
and expressive signs of simple and
compound concepts, and hence in
every language words are
distinguished in the same way as
things and concepts, insofar as
they are expressible and signifiable
by words.

Naturally, there were modistic counterarguments; Pinborg (1967) edits
some of them and discusses them at length. Aurifaber's arguments (and

those of his unknown contemporaries) were far from conclusive, but they did cause modistic grammarians to shift their attention from developing their theory to defending it. This may be the main reason – at least in the short run – why the development of modistic syntax came to such an abrupt halt. After all, Aurifaber's arguments, even if one accepts them, impugn only *modi significandi*, not *constructio*, *dependentia*, or the *primum–secundum* relation; he presents no serious objection to modistic syntax as distinct from modistic metatheory.

Such objections were, however, not long in coming. In his *Summa logicae*, written about 1323 and immensely influential at Oxford and Paris, William of Ockham develops the idea that mental language has its own syntax, which is not necessarily the same as that of written or spoken language:

Nam sicut vocum quaedam sunt nomina, quaedam sunt verba, quaedam sunt aliarum partium, ... et consimiliter est de scriptis, sic intentionum animae quaedam sunt nomina, quaedam verba, quaedam sunt aliarum partium, quia quaedam sunt pronomina, quaedam adverbia, quaedam coniunctiones, quaedam praepositiones.

Just as some spoken words are nouns and some are verbs, and some are other parts of speech, and the same is the case with written words, so some mental concepts are nouns, some are verbs, and some are other parts of speech – some are pronouns, some are adverbs, some are conjunctions, and some are prepositions.

Utrum autem participiis vocalibus et scriptis correspondeant in mente quaedam intentiones a verbis distinctae potest esse dubium ... nam verbum et participium verbi sumptum cum hoc verbo 'est' semper videntur in significando aequivalere ... ita videtur quod distinctio inter verba et participia non est propter necessitatem expressionis inventa, propter quod videtur quod non oportet participiis vocalibus distinctos conceptus in mente correspondere.

There is, however, room for doubt as to whether the mental concepts corresponding to spoken and written participles are distinct from those corresponding to verbs, for the verb seems always to mean the same thing as its participle taken with the verb 'is' [e.g., 'runs' = 'is running'], and so it seems that the distinction between spoken verbs and participles was not made because of any necessity of expression, for which reason it seems unnecessary

Et de pronominibus potest esse
consimilis dubitatio. (I.3, p. 11)

for there to be distinct concepts in
the mind corresponding to
participles in speech. A similar
doubt can be raised concerning
pronouns.

Ockham goes on to argue that not all the grammatical features (*accidentia grammaticalia*) of spoken words exist in mental language. Mental nouns, he says, have number and case – 'man', 'men', and 'man's' are different thoughts – but lack grammatical gender and morphological structure (*figura*). He admits as relevant to mental language only those *accidentia* that can change the truth-value of a proposition, and he notes that *homo est alba*, 'a man [masc.] is white [fem.]', while ungrammatical, is true under exactly the same conditions as the correct form *homo est albus*.

In a book titled *Destructiones modorum significandi* and written in the last years of the fourteenth century, Pierre d'Ailly goes further.[4] He argues that the concept of grammaticality, and not just truth-value, does apply to mental language – but mental grammaticality is not the same as spoken grammaticality. He states his position in the form of twelve conclusions:

(1) In orationibus mentalibus est congruitas.

(1) In mental sentences there is grammaticality.

(2) In orationibus mentalibus est vera et propria congruitas.

(2) In mental sentences there is true grammaticality in the proper sense of the term.

(3) In orationibus mentalibus est proprium regimen.

(3) In mental sentences there is government in the proper sense of the term.

(4) Congruitas, regimen et constructio sunt naturaliter in propositionibus mentalibus.

(4) Grammaticality, government, and syntactic structure exist in mental propositions by nature.

(5) Congruitas, regimen et constructio competunt orationi mentali per se et proprie.

(5) Grammaticality, government, and syntactic structure pertain to the mental sentence per se and in the proper sense of each term.

(6) Ista tria magis intrinsice conveniunt orationi mentali quam

(6) These three things pertain more intrinsically to the mental sentence

omni alteri orationi, quia
naturaliter conveniunt.

than to any other kind of sentence,
since they belong to it by nature.

(7) Propria constructio, propria
congruitas et proprium regimen
sunt in oratione mentali sine tali
modo significandi active vel
passive.

(7) Genuine syntactic structure,
grammaticality, and government,
in the strict sense of each term, are
present in the mental sentence
without any mode of signifying or
of being signified.

(8) Omne quod regitur vel regit in
oratione mentali naturaliter regit
vel regitur.

(8) Everything that participates in
grammatical government in the
mental sentence does so by nature.

(9) Sicut nominativus casus regitur
naturaliter, ita ... et generaliter
omnis casus in omni regimine ab
aliquo rectus.

(9) Just as the subject is linked to
the verb by nature, so generally
any case in any kind of
government is linked by nature to
whatever governs it.

(10) Praecisa causa quare aliqua
vox est nomen est ista, quia est
nota alicuius conceptus nominalis,
vel quia est nota alicuius nominis
mentalis, quod idem est.

(10) The exact reason why a
particular word is a noun is that it
is the representation of a noun-like
concept, or that it is the symbol
for a mental noun, which is the
same thing.

(11) Omne regimen communiter
usitatum vel est mentale, vocale
vel scriptum.

(11) Every generally recognized
government relation is either
mental, vocal, or written.

(12) Cuiuscumque regiminis
ultima vis ad quam reducitur est
conceptus. (Pinborg 1967: 204–5)

(12) The ultimate principle to
which every government relation
goes back is the concept.

By themselves, these conclusions can be interpreted as a tightly reasoned
plea for a purely semantic grammar – the Generative Semantics of its time,
so to speak – but in combination with Ockham's ideas, they point to what
must have been many people's conclusion: that studying the syntax of
natural language is no way to study cognition. The whole modistic metatheory, involving parallel modes of being, understanding, and signifying,
has been ruled out; the posited necessary connection between the structures

of reality, of cognition, and of language has been taken away; and the upshot of it all is that spoken or written language is not merely an indirect source of information about thought, but indeed a potentially misleading one. The right way to study cognition is to ignore Latin and Greek and study thought – that is, reasoning – itself; this is what the logicians who enthusiastically adopted Ockham's new terminism set out to do.

6.2 The modistic achievement

The Middle Ages were a period of progress for the study of syntax generally, and not all of this progress is attributable to the Modistae. The didactic grammarians are responsible for the theory of morphological *regimen* with all its embellishments: *regere a parte ante, a parte post, ex natura, ex vi* (see Thurot 1868:244–5). The pre-modistic speculative grammarians, such as Petrus Helias, developed referential *regimen* and produced theoretically interesting classifications of constructions.

Specifically modistic achievements comprise such things as the following:

(1) analysis of the whole of syntactic structure into dyadic linkages between elements, and use of the term *constructio* to refer to these linkages;
(2) further development of the concept of referential dependency, and its application to all types of constructions;
(3) formulation of the *primum–secundum* relation, and its use, along with referentially defined *dependentia*, to explicate the notion of transitivity;
(4) specific points of analysis, for instance the treatment of the antecedent–anaphor relation as a *constructio intransitiva*.

When we turn from the Modistae to the great Latin grammarians of the Renaissance, such as Linacre (1524), Despauterius (1537), Scaliger (1540), Ramus (1559, 1580), and Sanctius (1562, 1587), it is striking how little of the modistic model of syntax has survived. *Constructio* has lost its technical sense and again refers more or less to any group of connected words, as in Priscian; referential dependency and the *primum–secundum* relation are unheard of; and if anything medieval survives, it is morphological *regimen*, now usually contrasted with *concordantia*.[5] (Linacre [1524, fol. 52r] does retain the modistic distinction between *constructio transitiva* and *intransi-*

tiva and even classes the relation of anaphor to antecedent as *intransitiva*, but this is exceptional.)

There are several reasons why modistic syntax did not endure. For one thing, even during the height of the modistic era, the syntax was not the most widely studied part of the theory. For a student at Paris in the 1300s, to know about modes of signifying meant, as often as not, to know something of the metatheory and the *etymologia* (roughly the material surveyed in section 3.2 above), but not much *diasynthetica*. About a quarter of the many surviving manuscripts of Thomas of Erfurt lack the section on syntax altogether (Pinborg 1967:318), and when in 1322 Johannes Josse wrote a mnemonic poem to help students remember the outlines of modistic grammar, he, too, left off syntax.

Moreover, after the nominalist attack, some nominalists pursued a form of speculative grammar that retained the concept of *modus significandi* in attenuated form while dispensing with modistic syntactic theory. Ockham had already pointed out that nominalism does not forbid one to speak of modes of signifying so long as one does not attribute too much self-existent reality to them. He uses the term himself in the *Summa logicae* and explains:

Tertius modus principalis figurae dictionis est habens ortum ex diversitate modorum significandi diversarum dictionum quae videntur similes inter se, propter quod quandoque deceptus credit quod similiter est arguendum ex una dictione et ex alia . . .

The third principal form of word-fallacy is that which has its origin in the difference of modes of signifying between different words that seem to resemble each other, so that sometimes the person making the mistake thinks one should argue the same way from one as from the other . . .

Ad cuius intellectum sciendum quod modi significandi non sunt aliquae res additae ipsis dictionibus, advenientes eis, sed est metaphorica locutio, dicendo quod dictiones habent diversos modos significandi, quia per talem orationem intelligitur ista oratio, 'diversae dictiones diversimode significant illa quae significant.' (III.4.10, p. 798)

To understand this, you should know that modes of signifying are not some kind of extra things added to the words themselves, over and above what makes them words; to say that words have modes of signifying is a metaphor-ical way of speaking, since by means of such a statement one understands this one: 'different words signify what they signify in different ways.'

(The fallacy that Ockham is talking about is rather broadly defined, but includes such things as arguing that 'whatever runs is a physical object; a man quickly runs; therefore a-man-quickly is a physical object' [p. 805].)

Pinborg (1967:195–7) cites a few examples of grammars that follow, or at least mention, this principle; but the most striking example I have come across, and one not heretofore noted, is the *Expositio Donati nominalis* printed at Rouen by Robert Mace in 1500. The title page describes the book as 'the famous exposition of Donatus according to the way of the Nominalists, dealing with questions about the parts of speech.'[6] The work is anonymous, and there is no indication of its date of origin except that, since it uses the word *modista*, it cannot be earlier than about 1350 (I suspect it is in fact a good bit later). The typeface and format suggest that Mace issued it as a companion volume to his edition of Josse, which contains an equally anonymous and undateable, though thoroughly modistic, commentary.

The author of the *Expositio Donati* is engaged in what might be called a determined effort to have things both ways – to save the useful parts of modistic metatheory (especially the idea that the parts of speech are defined not by what they signify, but by the way they signify it) while rejecting realist ontology. He criticizes Donatus' definition of the noun as 'a part of speech inflected for case, signifying a physical object or situation' ('Pars orationis significans cum casu corpus aut rem,' *Ars grammatica*, p. 354) as follows:[7]

A Prisciano nomen sic definitur: nomen est pars orationis quae unicuique subiectorum sive rerum propriam aut communem distinguit qualitatem, quae definitio est eadem cum definitione Donati, licet tamen sub aliis verbis detur. Sed nec illa nec ista Donati sunt definitiones essentiales ipsius nominis, cum nulla detur per essentialia seu modos essentiales partis, et ab auctore modorum significandi datur una definitio talis, ut 'nomen est pars orationis

Priscian defines the noun thus: 'A noun is a part of speech that distinguishes the individual or shared what-ness of one or more subjects or things' – which is the same as Donatus' definition, though stated in different words. But neither this nor the definition given by Donatus is the essential definition of the noun itself, since neither is stated in terms of the essential characteristics or essential modes of that part of speech. The author of the Modes

significans per modum substantiae determinatae,' et ista est definitio essentialis nominis ... Et in praedicta definitio ponitur pars loco generis et totum residuum circumloquitur differentiam essentialem causalem ipsius nominis. (fol. 3va)

of Signifying gives a definition such as 'a noun is a part of speech signifying through the mode of a determinate substance,' and this is the essential definition of the noun. And in the definition given earlier, the part of speech is treated as a genus, and all the rest is an indirect way of indicating the essential difference that makes the noun a noun.

He follows this with a thoroughly modistic-sounding exposition of the difference between accidental and essential modes, but explains that 'essential modes are those expressed by the terms in the essential definitions of the parts of speech' [8] – that is, neither the mode of signifying nor its essentialness exists in any objective sense; describing something as 'essential' is only a shorthand way of saying that it plays a criterial role in the statement of a definition.

Again. he gives definitions of the cases that are practically copied from Thomas of Erfurt (*Grammatica speculativa*, pp. 186–92), but with a nominalistic caveat appended:

Notandum est tertio quod dictionibus mentalibus pluralitas casuum reperitur ex natura conceptus repraesentativi rei. Unde omnis conceptus casualis repraesentativus rei vel repraesentat rem recte vel oblique ... Si oblique, vel per modum 'ut cuius,' et sic est genitivus, vel per modum 'ut cui,' et sic est dativus, vel per modum 'ut ad quem,' et sic est accusativus, vel per modum 'ut a quo,' et sic est ablativus. Nolo tamen in proposito dicere quod illi modi significandi sint distincti a

Third, note that mental words have a variety of cases because of the nature of the concept that represents the thing referred to. Hence every case-marked concept that represents a real-world object represents it in either a non-oblique or an oblique case ... If in an oblique case, then either through the mode 'of which,' and so it is genitive, or through the mode 'to which,' and so it is dative, or through the mode 'toward which,' and so it is accusative, or through the mode

terminis significantibus; immo
sunt ipsimet termini significantes.
(fol. 27rb)

'from which,' and so it is ablative.
Nonetheless, I do not wish to say
on this matter that those modes of
signifying are anything distinct
from the meaning-bearing terms;
on the contrary, [as far as
existence is concerned] they are the
meaning-bearing terms themselves.

One striking fact about the *Expositio Donati nominalis* is that the modistic model of sentence structure is quite absent from it. The fact that the work is a commentary on Donatus means, of course, that there is no section explicitly devoted to syntax, for Donatus himself has none; but this does not prevent the author from tackling occasional syntactic problems, and when he does, his approach is basically that of the pre-modistic *regimen* theorists. For example:

Omnis comparativus natus est
regere genitivum a parte post.
Patet conclusio, nam omnis
comparativus gradus natus est
poni partitive ... ut patet per
Alexandrum dicentem 'Pone
gradum medium partitivo' et
cetera. (fol. 13vb)

Every comparative is inherently
capable of governing a genitive *a
parte post*. This conclusion is
obvious, since every comparative
is inherently capable of being used
as a partitive, as is evident from
Alexander de Villa Dei, who says
'Use the middle grade as a
partitive' and so forth [*Doctrinale*,
line 1175].

For a Modista to cite the *Doctrinale* as a syntactic authority would have been a little unusual – rather like a modern linguist citing a desktop dictionary on a point of semantics. But in the succeeding discussion, the author of the *Expositio* cites Alexander again; more importantly, he makes it clear that, like some pre-modistic grammarians such as Hugh of St Victor, he believes that *regimen* is caused by semantic relation.

Quilibet comparativus simpliciter
et partitive tentus virtute suae
significationis natus est regere a
parte post ablativum singularem

Every comparative, by itself and
taken partitively, is by virtue of its
meaning intrinsically capable of
governing an ablative singular or

vel pluralem sine praepositione ...	plural *a parte post* without a preposition ...
Dicitur etiam notanter 'virtute suae significationis' ratione cuius quandoque regit alium casum ...	I make a point of saying 'by virtue of its meaning,' by virtue of which it sometimes governs another case instead ...
Unde ulterius notandum est quod omne nomen positivi gradus sufficit regere ablativum sui absoluti ex vi effectus causae formalis. Probatur, quia talis ablativus significat causam formalem rei per positivum ut 'albedo' significat causam formalem ipsius albi, ut satis patet ex Alexandro capitulo de regimine albativi; patet etiam ex modo dicendo sic, 'iste est coloratus colore', 'iste est albus albedine' [etc.]. (fol. 13vb–14ra)	Hence, finally, one should note that every noun [adjective] of positive degree is capable of governing the ablative of the noun substantive that refers to the same thing, by virtue of the effect of a formal cause. The proof of this is that such an ablative signifies the formal cause of the thing referred to by the positive adjective, as 'whiteness' signifies the formal cause of a white thing, as is evident from Alexander in his chapter on the *regimen* of the ablative [1288 ff.]; moreover, it is evident from locutions such as 'it is colored with [such-and-such] a color', 'it is white with whiteness', and so forth.

For a nominalist, of course, the modes of signifying are merely ways of looking at or describing meaning, not entities distinct from it, and hence the question of whether construction is caused by meaning or by modes of signifying does not have the same significance that it had for the Modistae.

But to blame the lack of survival of modistic syntax entirely on the nominalist attack would be to exaggerate the influence that modism had exerted before the attack took place. Even at the height of its popularity, modistic grammar had come nowhere near dominating the teaching of Latin. It was a theoretical discipline, analogous to transformational grammar rather than English composition at a modern university. Modism was normally quite absent from the elementary classroom, and schoolboys learned to construct Latin sentences with the aid of the *Doctrinale* and similar works (see Paetow 1910). The few known exceptions, such as the *Fundamentum puerorum* of Thomas of Erfurt, date only from a brief period when the Modistae were at the height of their prominence; and there were many places, such as Oxford and Cambridge, where modistic grammar scarcely caught on even among the theoreticians.

Moreover, modistic grammar was by nature not very suitable for elementary teaching. From the teacher's point of view, it was much more important that syntactic analyses should be easy to carry out – and easy to teach students to carry out – than that they should express deep insights about the nature of language. From this standpoint, the *primum–secundum* and referential dependency relations are far too difficult and problematic to use in the classroom, whereas morphological *regimen*, though less elegantly defined, is from a practical point of view ideal. So however successful the modistic model may have been in terms of its original theory-oriented goals, it had nothing to commend it to those who believed that the only reason for studying grammar was to learn to write good Latin.

Hence the coming of the humanist era marked the complete demise of modistic syntax. By 1418, Guarino Veronese had published his influential *Regulae grammaticales*, containing what Percival (1975:239) describes as 'a medieval syntax with certain crucial components excised' – in particular, transitivity and all grammatical relations except *regimen* were gone – and by the beginning of the sixteenth century, Despauterius was classifying the semantic values of various kinds of *regimen* in much the same way as Hugh of St Victor had done four hundred years earlier.[9] Grammarians had, for the moment, lost interest in the nature of syntactic structure; when they regained it, too much time and too much philosophical polemizing had come between them and the Modistae for the modistic achievement to be properly appreciated.

Appendix: Notes on certain questions of authorship

The authorship of most medieval grammatical treatises is uncertain; quite often nothing is known about the author of a treatise except what can be inferred from internal evidence. This appendix comprises a set of notes giving information about particularly obscure authors, explaining how I have dealt with treatises that have been attributed to more than one author in the modern literature, and, where applicable, presenting additional evidence bearing on questions of authorship.

In general, I have referred to authors by the names by which they are known to modern scholars, even when such names represent uncertain inferences. When a treatise has long been attributed to an author but the weight of the evidence is now against that attribution, I have prefixed 'Pseudo-' to the traditional author's name. In a couple of cases I have used names assigned by Pinborg, consisting of 'Anonymus' followed by the present location of the manuscript (which is not necessarily where the medieval author was active).

A.1 Anonymus Norimbergensis

This is Pinborg's name for the otherwise unknown author or authors of two series of *Quaestiones super Priscianum minorem* (treating books XVII and XVIII respectively) that are found in Nuremberg Stadtbibliothek manuscript Cent.V.21, fol. 31r–34v and 35r–53r. The two series are written in the same hand and represent the same doctrinal milieu (that of Radulphus Brito, Thomas of Erfurt, and the other late Parisian Modistae); it is not known whether they are in fact the work of a single author.

The significance of the treatises was pointed out by Pinborg (1980b: 204–6), who presented a transcription and translation of one interesting passage. I have used my own transcription and translation of the same material, not because of any deficiencies on the part of Pinborg's, but purely to attain greater consistency with my treatment of other material from the same manuscript.

A.2 Johannes le Rus

The *Summa de arte grammatica* of Johannes le Rus is known in three manuscripts, of which Vatican Library ms. Vat. Lat. 7678, fol. 89r–101v is the only one I have examined in detail and the only one that gives the author's name. (The author is called Johannes *de* Rus by Grabmann (1940) and Pinborg (1967), apparently as a result of misreading the heading on the manuscript.)

Johannes le Rus was probably a professor at the Faculty of Arts in Paris in or just before the middle of the thirteenth century. He seems to have been an Englishman, or at least to have had connections with England; in the Vatican manuscript, the *explicit* of his grammatical *Summa* refers to him as Johannes Anglus (fol. 101v), and the second part of the *sophisma* collection preceding it, which Grabmann attributes to the same author, begins 'In ista parte tractandum est a nobis de intellectu distinctionum ... quod magno labore diligenti animo a diversarum nationum magistris Parisiis *et in Anglia* memoriae commendavimus' (Grabmann 1940:34, emphasis mine).

A.3 Jordanus

Sirridge (1980) has edited a *Priscianus minor* commentary that, to judge from its contents, dates from the early thirteenth century (before Kilwardby); two manuscripts give the name of its author as Jordanus. In 1940 Martin Grabmann suggested that the author was Jordanus of Saxony (d. 1237), who is known to have written a commentary on *Priscianus minor*.

However, Sirridge (1980:v–vi) is skeptical about this identification, mainly because of internal evidence that the author of this treatise, unlike Jordanus of Saxony, also wrote a commentary on *Priscianus maior*. I have therefore referred to the author of this treatise simply as Magister Jordanus, leaving the question open.

A.4 Kilwardby

The English Dominican Robert Kilwardby (d. 1279), author of the *De ortu scientiarum* and many other well-known works, is known to have written the *Priscianus minor* commentary 'Sicut dicit Aristoteles in secundo de anima ... ' Commonly associated with this is a *Priscianus maior* commentary, also attributed to Kilwardby, selected passages from which have been edited by Fredborg, Green-Pedersen, Nielsen, and Pinborg (1975). In an article on 'The problem of the authorship' printed as pp. 12–17 of the introductory matter for that edition, Osmund Lewry, OP, expresses considerable doubt that Kilwardby is the real author. The formats of the *Priscianus maior* and *minor* commentaries are rather different, certainly more different than one would expect if they had been written as a two-volume set by one author. Moreover, the author of the *maior* commentary uses a classification of the sciences rather different from Kilwardby's; most strikingly, the *maior* commentary insists that grammar is a speculative science (pp. 30–2), while Kilwardby strongly suggests that it is *practica* or else *adminiculativa* (*De ortu scientiarum*, chapters 45–7), a view that the *maior* commentary attributes to 'quosdam' (p. 13).

Particularly in view of this striking discrepancy about the status of grammar as a science, I have concluded that the weight of the evidence is against attributing the *Priscianus maior* commentary to Kilwardby and have therefore referred to its author as Pseudo-Kilwardby.

A.5 Petrus Croccus

Manuscript 1142 of the Bibliothèque de Troyes contains a commentary on the *Doctrinale* of Alexander de Villa Dei. The commentary is a treasury of information on early modistic syntactic theory, in particular because the author is placed in the position of having to compare his own theory with the older didactic grammar of the work on which he is commenting.

The commentary is immense; it fills 185 leaves (370 pages) and is written in a small hand with extensive use of abbreviations. Transcribed into ordinary modern print, it would fill roughly a thousand pages.

Pinborg (1967:86n) identifies the author on the basis of the colophon, 'Explicunt notulae compositae a magistro Petro Crocco et a magistro Petro de Herunco in Alvernia quae apud Divionem fuerunt recitatae seu reportatae,' and cites two unedited treatises that refer to this treatise as the work of 'Petrus de Crocco,' indicating that he, and not Petrus de Herunco, was the principal author. He goes on to identify Petrus Croccus tentatively as Pierre le Croq, a master of theology active in the late thirteenth century. Doctrinally, the treatise resembles Boethius Dacus and Martin of Dacia and can therefore be dated circa 1275.

A.6 Simon Dacus

The attribution of the *Domus grammaticae* and the *Quaestiones super secundum minoris voluminis Prisciani* to Simon Dacus goes back to the manuscript catalogue compiled by Amplonius in 1412, and both works are given in Otto's 1963 edition (*Simonis Daci opera*). However, as Pinborg (1967:95–7) has pointed out, it is obvious from the doctrinal content that these two works represent quite different stages in the development of medieval grammar: the *Domus* is pre-modistic, while the *Quaestiones* display modistic grammar in mature form. On the basis of content the two works can be dated circa 1250/70 and circa 1280/90 respectively. Moreover, Pinborg (p. 96) notes that there are more Germanisms in the Latin of the *Domus* than in that of the *Quaestiones*.

The evidence is very strong that these treatises were written by different authors, whom I propose to call Simon Dacus Domifex (author of the *Domus*) and Simon Dacus Modista (author of the *Quaestiones* and, in all probability, of the unedited Martin of Dacia commentary 'Rhetoricae primo scribitur a philosopho "Turpe est ignorare ..." ' [A 25 in the indices of Pinborg 1967]).

Notes

(There are no notes to Chapter 1.)

2: Before the Modistae

[1] He does not really make it clear *why* all sets are fully ordered – he seems to think the only alternative is to hold that all sets are unordered, which would be absurd. 'Quidam suae solacium imperitiae quaerentes aiunt, non oportere de huiuscemodi rebus quaerere, suspicantes fortuitas esse ordinationum positiones. Sed quantum ad eorum opinionem, evenit generaliter nihil per ordinationem accipi nec contra ordinem peccari, quod existimare penitus stultum. Si autem in quibusdam concedant esse ordinationem, necesse est etiam omnibus eam concedere' (XVII.12). This is practically a word-for-word translation of Apollonius (*On Syntax* I.13), who has nothing to add by way of justification for the position.

[2] Apollonius and Priscian seem never to have considered the idea of a *partially* ordered set, even though a partial ordering is all they actually give arguments for.

[3] By *accentus* Priscian probably means 'tone'; elsewhere he tries to apply the Greek accents (i.e., tones) to Latin (II.12 et passim).

[4] Whether or not it is a morpheme: *praemium, praetor, praelum*. Presumably Priscian would not consider *repraehendo* a counterexample to this generalization, since for him *re* and *prae* are prepositions and hence count as separate words.

[5] *Transitio personarum* is, of course, Apollonius' concept of διάβασις τοῦ προσώπου (*On Syntax* III.14, Περὶ ἀντωνυμίας pp. 45–8). Neither Apollonius nor Priscian gives a systematic exposition of the concept; it is brought up and explained briefly at various points in connection with other things.

[6] Perhaps this enigmatic sentence is a literal translation of something in Apollonius' (now lost) book on the preposition, which Priscian appears to be following at this point.

[7] Quoted by Thurot (1868:17), Hunt (1943:211, in English paraphrase), Roos (1952:93), Robins (1967:76, 91; 1974:15), and others. A complete but corrupt text of the *De philosophia mundi*, which is mostly about astronomy and cosmology, is edited in the *Patrologia Latina* (vol. 172, columns 39–102), erroneously attributed to Honorius Augustodunensis. The best text of the paragraph from which I quote is given by Jeauneau (1960:218).

[8] This reconciliation corresponds almost point-by-point to that given by Boethius (*Commentarii in librum Aristotelis 'Peri hermeneias,' editio secunda*, ed. Meiser, vol.

2, pp. 14–15), who warns the reader not to take Aristotle to task (*calumniari*) for not treating all the parts of speech.

[9] The date of circa 1170 proposed by de Rijk (1967) is no longer generally accepted. (K. M. Fredborg, personal communication. She provides the following reference, which I myself have not been able to examine: Klaus Jacobi, 'Wilhelm von Shyreswood und die Dialectica Monacensis,' in *English Logic and Semantics* [*Aristarium, Supplementum* 1], Nijmegen: Ingermann Publishers, 1981, pp. 99–130.)

[10] *Subiectum* and *praedicatum* remained terms of logic, not of grammar, throughout the Middle Ages.

[11] For example: 'Nam substantiam alicuius suppositi quaerentes dicimus, "Quis movetur? Quis ambulat? Quis loquitur?"' (Priscian, *Institutiones* XVII.23). See Ebbesen (1981), who argues against de Rijk's suggestion (1967:521) that *suppositum* had meant 'grammatical subject' since the early Middle Ages.

[12] I have made no attempt to trace the complete history of *regimen*; the set of medieval authors I draw on should be regarded as no more than a sampling of those who are at present relatively well known.

[13] Much interesting background information on these and other didactic grammarians is given by Murphy (1974:135–93).

[14] *Regere* is not the only term; *gubernare* and *poscere* are quite common as synonyms for it, and one finds a number of others, particularly in verse grammars.

[15] 'Noun' of course comprises adjectives as well as substantives.

[16] Hugh gives only the governing nouns; I have supplied appropriate genitives in the examples quoted.

[17] In the words of Steinthal (quoted by Robins 1980:232), worse than muddled: 'Priscians Bericht ist erst verstümmelt und dann verwirrt worden.'

[18] Many medieval grammarians give summaries of what Priscian says about Stoic grammar – particularly commentators on Alexander de Villa Dei, *Doctrinale*, line 1501, which mentions *asymbama* – but no one, so far as I can determine, makes any effort to expand on Priscian's brief account.

[19] In an appendix to his *Priscianus minor* commentary, pp. 153–8.

[20] The anachronism entailed by a sentence such as this does not seem to have bothered the medieval grammarians. In the twelfth to the fourteenth centuries the stock *dramatis personae* of the example sentences – analogous to the transformationalists' *John* and *Bill* – were *Socrates* (often abbreviated *Sor* or *Sortes*), *Plato*, *Vergilius*, and, often, the given name of the lecturer himself (e.g., *Petrus* in Petrus Helias and *Thomas* in Thomas of Erfurt).

[21] William of Conches, *De philosophia mundi*, column 100: 'Ordo vero discendi talis est ut, quia per eloquentiam omnis sit doctrina, prius instruatur in eloquentia. Cuius sunt tres partes, recte scribere, et recte pronuntiare scripta, quod confert grammatica; probare quod probandum est, quod docet dialectica; ornare verba et sententias, quod tradit rhetorica.'

Throughout this section I am heavily indebted to Pinborg (1967:21–30).

[22] This is a summary of *Posterior Analytics* I.4, 73 a 21–74 a 3.

[23] On Alfarabi see also Mahdi 1975, who gives an excellent summary of the *Liber de scientiis* in English.

3: Modistic grammar

[1] Many of the Modistae did original work in both grammar and logic while keeping the two fields clearly distinct, in much the same way as a present-day linguist might do research in both syntax and phonology. Modistic grammar was of course much more influential than modistic logic, on which see Pinborg (1975a). Extensive modistic influence is evident in the logic of Duns Scotus, among others.

[2] Some modern scholars have applied the term 'Modistae' more broadly to all medieval grammarians who used the term *modus significandi*. I am following Pinborg in restricting it to those who applied modism to syntax as well as *etymologia*.

[3] The author of the *Domus grammaticae*; the earlier of the two authors previously thought to be a single author by the name of Simon Dacus. See the Appendix.

[4] 'Ein Meisterwerk der neuen Gattung, und zwar vor allem ein pädagogisches Meisterwerk' (Pinborg 1967:67).

[5] Pinborg, personal communication.

[6] Pinborg, personal communication. The *Quaestiones* are, after all, unattested in manuscript, so all that we know from external evidence is that they date from before 1496, the date of the first printed edition. The first two of the *Quaestiones Alberti* read like slightly condensed versions of the corresponding Questions of Radulphus Brito (c. 1300), while the rest reflect an earlier, less sophisticated version of modistic theory. This suggests that the *Quaestiones Alberti* are a compilation of two of Radulphus' Questions together with some older material, rather than a source from which Radulphus extracted two Questions while ignoring the rest.

[7] There have been numerous printed editions of Thomas's work; the most recent is that of Bursill-Hall (1972). Earlier editions usually attribute the work to Duns Scotus, and it appears in Wadding's edition of Scotus' *Opera omnia* (Lyons, 1639, vol. 1, pp. 45–76).

Intending only to give the textus receptus, Bursill-Hall retains Wadding's rather corrupt text, which he gets at second hand and in somewhat altered form from an edition issued by Fernández García in 1902; no one since Wadding has produced an edition based on manuscript work. A list of suggested emendations to Bursill-Hall's text was published by Pinborg (1974), but this only scratches the surface. In addition to consulting several manuscripts on various points, I have found the 1489 Deventer incunabulum particularly helpful in emending corrupt passages.

[8] Edited by Gansiniec (1960: 105–6). It is a brief mnemonic poem.

[9] Edited by Gansiniec (1960: 149–54). Kelly has informed me that the date of '1300?' given for this treatise in one of his articles (Kelly 1979: 164, 178) is the result of a typographical error. Johannes Stobnicensis or John of Stobniczy (1470–1518) is a relatively well-known figure, and even if he is not the author, the treatise could not have been written before the late fourteenth century at the earliest, since it uses the term *Modistae*, which did not come into use until modism was under attack; moreover, there was no university at Cracow until 1364.

[10] Actually, the 'Proprium est' series (II.18–21) is a list of distinguishing features only; a fuller definition is given at the beginning of Priscian's discussion of each part of speech individually, but these fuller definitions are no less heterogeneous.

[11] See Pinborg (1967:27, 35), who cites Nicholas of Paris and Goswin of Marbais (both circa 1250).

[12] See also Pseudo-Albertus, *Quaestiones* 1, pp. 4–5, and Boethius Dacus, pp. 263–4. The treatment of this problem was an issue in pre-modistic speculative grammar (see for instance Kilwardby, quoted by Thurot, 1868:125–6, and Pseudo-Kilwardby, pp. 106–7) but had become conventionalized by the time of the Modistae.

[13] *De interpretatione* 2–3, 16 a 20 – 16 b 12.

[14] Boethius, *Commentarii in librum Aristotelis 'Peri hermeneias,' editio secunda*, ed. Meiser, p. 57. His choice of words may have contributed something to the eventual rise of the term *modus significandi*.

[15] It is sometimes said that the term 'speculative grammar' refers to the way language was thought to be a mirror (*speculum*) of the structure of the real world. However, I have found no evidence that this is so. The Modistae used the term *speculativa* only to mean 'theoretical' (see section 2.4 above).

[16] Boethius Dacus points out that the failure of tenseless verbs to occur in attested languages – at least, in those known to the Modistae – makes no difference: 'Et tu dicis, quod nullum invenimus verbum, quod caret tempore; dico quod hoc non cogit, quia nec omnia possibilia invenimus in actu' (*Quaestiones* 84, 'Utrum verbum possit privari tempore,' p. 201).

[17] See Enders and Pinborg's edition. The marginal notes are in the Nuremberg manuscript.

[18] The relation of modism to realist ontology is the principal concern of Pinborg's *Die Entwicklung der Sprachtheorie im Mittelalter* (1967); Bursill-Hall (1971) gives a detailed survey of the structure of the terminological system.

[19] This type of diagram was first used by Bursill-Hall (1963, 1971:348).

[20] That this is the correct translation is made clear by Siger de Courtrai: 'Modus autem significandi ... est duplex, quidam activus et quidam passivus, quia, secundum quod dicit Priscianus in maiore volumine, quotiescumque ab aliquo verbo descendit gerundium desinens in -*di*, significat duo, scilicet actionem et passionem' (p. 42). That is, the terms *activus* and *passivus* were added to make up for the inability of Latin to distinguish active and passive gerunds. The translations 'active mode of signifying' and 'passive mode of signifying' are at best unclear and at worst positively misleading; I do not recommend their use.

[21] For a clear exposition of this system see Thomas of Erfurt, *Grammatica speculativa* 1–10, pp. 134–6. It used to be thought that Siger of Courtrai included an extra layer of *modi signandi* between the *modi significandi* and the *modi intelligendi*, but this has now been shown to have been purely a conjecture made by Wallerand to resolve some corruptions in a text he was editing (see Siger, ed. Pinborg, pp. 34–5).

[22] 'Omnis enim constructio, quam Graeci σύνταξιν vocant, ad intellectum vocis est reddenda,' *Institutiones* XVII.187.

[23] 'Quandoque congrua est voce et non sensu dictionum ordinatio, ... veluti quando nomen adiectivum secundae positionis iungitur substantivo primae positionis, ut si dicam, "Socrates habet hypotheticos sotulares cum categoricis corrigiis," congrue iunguntur dictiones quantum ad vocem, sed ex his nihil habet

auditor quod rationaliter intelligere possit,' Petrus Helias, p. 1. *Prima* and *secunda* *(im)positio* are object language and metalanguage respectively.

[24] The two passages quoted occur in the opposite order in the text.

[25] '[Principium efficiens constructionis] intrinsecum sunt modi significandi respectivi, ratione quorum vel unum constructibile est ad alterum dependens, vel alterius dependentiam determinans [i.e., terminans]; a quibus modis significandi respectivis abstrahuntur duo modi significandi generales, scilicet modus dependendi in uno constructibili et modus dependentiam terminans in altero constructibili,' *Grammatica speculativa* 89, p. 274. On the full meaning of *dependere* and *terminare* see section 4.4.

[26] Radulphus Brito (I.17) reviews the whole issue in detail.

[27] For a more extensive exegesis of Thomas's text, see Covington (1979). I no longer agree with the interpretation of the *dependens–terminans* relation given there.

[28] In using 'white' as their standard sample adjective, the Modistae are echoing Aristotle, one of whose categories is 'quality, such as "white" or "literate"' (ποιὸν δὲ οἷον λευκόν, γραμματικόν, IV, I b 30; Anselm in writing *De grammatico* chose the other one), and who uses 'white' in his classic examples of contraries and contradictories ('Every man is white/not every man is white,' etc., *De interpretatione* VIII, 18 a 13–17). (See also *Prior Analytics* I.3, 25 b 11–14 et passim.)

[29] Some of the Modistae, such as Martin of Dacia and Siger de Courtrai, make no use of this distinction. It is present in the work of Petrus Helias (ed. Tolson, p. 58), Robert Blund (c. 1175–1200), and Alexander de Villa Dei (1199?), though they apply it only to transitive constructions. On its extension to intransitive constructions, see Thurot (1868:233), who cites Kilwardby.

I am indebted to K. M. Fredborg for the use of her transcription of the first few pages of Robert Blund, *Summa in arte grammatica*, British Library ms. Royal 2.D.XXX fol. 79r ff. An edition of Blund by C. H. Kneepkens is in preparation.

[30] This sentence is a made-up illustration.

4: Syntactic structure

[1] A typical case is Petrus Croccus' claim that just as real-world objects are 'constructed' out of earth, air, fire, and water, so too grammatical constructions ought to be composed of various elements with contrary properties:

> Circa istud capitulum (*Doctrinale* 1369 ff.) potest quaeri in generali utrum constructio sit possibilis, et arguitur quod non. Philosophus dicit in secundo Physicorum quod sicut est in natura ita est in arte; sed omne compositum naturale est compositum per diversas proprietates, sicut homo compositus ex quattuor elementis, et omne compositum fit ex terra, aqua, aëre, et igne, et ita habent diversas proprietates, ut patet: aqua est humida et frigida, ignis est calidus et siccus. Ergo ita erit in compositis artis. Cum ergo constructio sit compositum artificiale, apparet quod componitur ex partibus habentibus oppositas proprietates. Sed non potest componi ex partibus habentibus diversas proprietates nisi componatur ex diversis constructibilibus hanentibus diversos modos significandi, et sic construeretur numerus singularis cum numero plurali, et hoc esset congrua: 'homo currunt'. Sed hoc est inconveniens, ergo constructio non potest esse.

To anyone not realizing that the arguments at the beginning of a Question are mostly straw men, much of medieval philosophy can appear quite ridiculous.

[2] For instance, he applies it to whole sentences in the discussion of Stoic terms quoted in section 2.3 above.

[3] Hugh of St Victor, *De grammatica*, p. 106; Petrus Helias, p. 1; Johannes le Rus, Vatican ms., fol. 91vb; Martin of Dacia, pp. 87–8.

[4] 'Ad primum quando dicitur "illa constructio requirit plura constructibilia duobus, in qua est dependentia mediata," verum est, non tanquam principalia, sed duo tantum tanquam principalia, scilicet per se dependens et per se terminans. Unde cum dicitur "vado ad ecclesiam", hic sunt duo constructibilia principalia, scilicet "vado" quod est dependens et "ecclesiam" quod est dependentiam terminans. Sed praepositio quae est medium dependendi unius ad alterum reducitur ad naturam terminantis dependentiam, scilicet casualis,' I.8, p. 116.

[5] The argument:

Omnis constructio ordinatur ad exprimendum conceptum mentis compositum. Sed una dictio sufficienter potest exprimere mentis conceptum compositum ... quia dictiones compositae ut 'impius', 'armiger', 'dapifer' significant mentis conceptum compositum. (p. 114)

Radulphus' reply:

Ad minorem 'una dictio' etc., dico quod duplex est conceptus compositus: quidam enim est conceptus compositus cadens circa significationem unius dictionis et ille significatur per unam dictionem quae significat sub conceptu composito, a quo accipitur figura composita vel decomposita. Quidam vero est conceptus compositus cadens circa diversa significata diversarum dictionum ... (p. 118)

The crucial point is that a true construction has *diversa significata*, whereas a compound word does not.

[6] Or, to put it in modistic terms, *impositio* and *constructio* differ in that *impositio* is done by few people – one prehistoric person, in the idealization with which the Modistae worked – while *constructio* is carried out by everyone.

[7] 'Omnis constructio transitione et intransitione completur,' p. 106.

[8] 'Exigere est, ut dicit P[etrus] H[elias], trahere dictionem in constructionem ad perfectionem orationis ex respectu transitivo ... Regere est dictioni determinatum casum conferre,' p. 67.

[9] 'Regimen est unio dictionis artificialis secundum concordantiam significatorum vel consignificatorum generalium,' p. 53.

[10] 'Cum autem dividatur constructio sicut constrictibile dividitur, dividitur autem constructibile in declinabile et in indeclinabile, necesse est quod dividatur constructio penes ordinationem declinabilium inter se, vel indeclinabilium inter se, vel indeclinabilium ad declinabilia. Ordinatio autem declinabilium ad indeclinabilia potest se habere tripliciter, quoniam aut indeclinabile erit determinatio declinabilis vel declinabile indeclinabilis vel utroque modo. Quod autem indeclinabile sit determinatio declinabilis, hoc accidit in constructione adverbiorum ad verba ut cum dicitur "Socrates currit nunc." Determinatur enim consignificatio temporis in verbo per adverbium,' and so on (Vatican ms., fol. 91vb, with emendations from the corresponding passage in the British Museum manuscript).

[11] 'Ad evidentiam huius quaestionis, quaedam sunt praemittenda: primo quid sit regere, et consequenter alia. Regere est secum trahere aliam dictionem [*dictionis*, ms.] ad perfectionem [*perfectionis*, ms.] orationis. Et postea reportatur quia ita

sequeretur quod ibi non esset regimen, "cappa Socratis", proper hoc, quod est imperfecta, sed solum in "cappa Socratis est bona". Hoc falsum est, quare et cetera.

Propter hoc definitur aliter: regere est conferre dictioni poni in tali casu et cogere eam virtualiter sic esse. Et quare dicitur hoc videamus consequenter.

Item debemus scire quid sit causa regiminis sive constructionis, quia pro eodem accipio "regimen" et "constructionem" quantum ad istam quaestionem ... Item constructio est congrua dictionum ordinatio ex modis significandi causata, et quia intentio facta est de modis significandi, ideo videamus [*videtur*, ms.] aliquid de modis significandi. Unum debemus scire: quod modus significandi nihil aliud est quam maneries significandi, sicut "homo" significat sub ista manerie quae est singularis numeri et masculini generis, et ista maneries potest dici "accidens consignificatum" et "modus significandi acciden⟨tali⟩s" quia accidit parti. "Consignificatum" appellatur quia hoc quod est "homo" habet hominem [ut] principalem significatum et cum hoc significat numerum singularem [et] nominativum casum ... Hoc dicitur et generaliter intelligitur; quando dicunt ita "constructio fit ratione consignificatorum" intelligendum est "ratione modorum significandi,"' fol. 77rl. Note the remarkably smooth, and complete, transition from glossing a technical term of school-grammar to dealing with a complex modistic theoretical issue.

[12] 'In grammatica illa dictio dicitur regere aliam, quae dirigit et gubernat aliam ad suum finem, qui finis est stare in tali casu' (Simon, p. 131); 'illud constructibile regit alterum sicut ex ea parte ex qua cogit ipsum stare in tali casu in quo ponitur, ita quod non in alio' (Anonymus Norimbergensis, Nuremberg Stadtbibliothek ms. Cent.V.21, fol. 50va).

[13] 'Ideo in grammatica dicitur quod quaedam regunt et non reguntur, et sic in qualibet oratione sive perfecta sive imperfecta semper dignius regit minus dignum. Est ergo regere in grammatica actus rationis qui attribuitur dictioni sub ratione qua regit aliam vel alias ad rectum finem habendum videlicet ad exprimendum conceptus mentis congrue et debito modo. Verum tamen grammatici antiqui ponebant quod regere est conferre dictioni poni in tali casu in quo debet stare, ita quod regimen attribuebant casibus, quod non debet fieri propter causam supradictam. Ideo partes indeclinabiles dicebantur ab ipsis neque regere neque regi, quod non est verum, ut patebit in alio sophismate, "O magister". Nomina autem appellativa dicebant regere et regi, ut "cappa Socratis", et in hoc bene ... nomina vero propria dicebant regi et non regere, quod non est verum quia nomen proprium regit suum adiectivum. Sic ergo patet quid est regere,' pp. 51–2.

The *sophisma* 'O magister' does not in fact tackle this issue; it establishes that indeclinables enter into construction but does not use *regimen* terminology.

[14] In the passage quoted, the modern printed editions have 'tantum petit vel exigit ... tantum dat vel concedit.' *Terminum* is the reading of the Munich manuscript CLM 22294 (Pinborg 1974), Cambridge University Library ms. Dd.XII.46, Bodleian Library ms. 643, and the 1489 Deventer incunabulum.

[15] 'Unum extremorum in qualibet constructione se habet ut terminans et per se stans et ut potentiale constructibile, et aliud extremum quod habet se ut dependens est ut formale ... Vel dicendum quod constructibile dependens est magis formale constructibile, quia constructio causatur ex dependentia unius constructibilis ad

alterum. Quod ergo magis operatur ad formam orationis quae est unio constructibilium, hoc est constructibile formalius. Et hoc est dependens, ergo et cetera˙ (I.6, pp. 110, 111).

[16] Other modistic and pre-modistic writers identify *regimen* with *dependentia,* but without making it clear whether it is the *dependens* that governs the *terminans* or vice versa. See, for example, Simon Dacus Domifex (p. 58), Pseudo-Albertus (p. 116), and Radulphus Brito (I.6, p. 111).

[17] 'Licet hoc quod est *cappa* non dependeat inquantum subiectum, tamen ... dependet ad istum genitivum *Socratis* gratia huius habitudinis fundatae super ipsum, quae est habere se per modum "ut alterius"' (*Quaestiones,* p. 125).

[18] For more on the *motus* model see section 4.7 below.

[19] In defense of Martin, it should be pointed out that he was discussing only the subject, and he may have had in mind some way of getting around the problem that arises with object modifiers.

[20] 'Si secundum dependet ad primum, sic est constructio intransitiva ... Si autem primum constructibile dependet ad secundum, secundo non dependente ad primum, sed ad aliud a primo diversum, sic est transitiva,' Thomas of Erfurt, p. 282; 'sicut enim constructio intransitiva causatur ex dependentia posterioris ad prius, sic transitiva e converso causatur ex dependentia prioris ad posterius,' Radulphus Brito, II.3, p. 356; cf. also Simon Dacus Modista, *Quaestiones,* p. 117.

[21] Psalm 101:23 (102:22 in Protestant and Jewish usage).

[22] Martin of Dacia does occasionally use *ante–post* terminology in a way reminiscent of Thomas's (but not his own) use of *primum* and *secundum;* for example, he refers to the verb–adverb relation as a *constructio intransitiva a parte post* (pp. 106 ff.).

[23] Here and elsewhere in medieval grammatical and logical treatises, *li, ly,* or *le* is the French definite article, used (like Aristotle's τό) to indicate that the following word or phrase is being treated as an example; one translates it by putting the following word in quotes.

This is a particularly striking case of the way medieval philosophical discourse uses words to indicate things that we would indicate with typeface or punctuation; other examples are the use of *item* to mark the beginning of a paragraph or of an item in a list, and the use of *dicendum est* to mark the beginning of the author's response to a series of arguments he is attacking.

[24] The *secundum,* in modistic terminology, not the *dependens,* of course.

[25] 'Dicendum quod istae duae passiones, "congruum" et "perfectum," habent ordinationem, et perfectum supponit congruum' (p. 97).

[26] According to Aquinas, the relation of complementarity or proportionateness holds not only between cause and effect, but also between matter and form, between motion and the thing that moves, between agent and patient, and even between creature and Creator (*In III Sententiarum* 1.1.1).

[27] In what follows I am expounding the contents of Martin of Dacia's *Modi significandi,* pp. 97–100 and 109–12.

[28] Martin (p. 98) cites Aristotle, *De interpretatione* I (16 b 25), which says that the copula ('is') signifies a mere σύνθεσις (*compositio*) that makes no assertion apart

from the things it links. In this context, Aristotle's implicit point is that most verbs (such as his example ὑγιαίνει, 'is healthy') function like a copula plus the thing that the copula links to the subject.

[29] On this point a couple of corrections to printed texts are in order. In Pseudo-Kilwardby's statement, which the editors give as 'oportet enim quod persona respondeat personae et numerus numero, sicut modus ⟨modo et casus⟩ casui' (p. 97), the interpolation is unnecessary; the text should read '. . . sicut modus casui.'

Also, at the beginning of section 226, p. 99, of Martin of Dacia's *Modi significandi*, 'modus significandi finitus' should probably read 'modus finitus,' which makes it slightly clearer that what is being referred to is finite mood; but the difference between the two wordings is not crucial, and there may have been confusion over it from the outset. (I have not been able to consult any manuscripts on this point.)

[30] To quote Abelard (who of course antedates terminism in the strict sense): 'Hos [i.e., *homo* + *est* + *animal*] quoque terminos propositionis categoricae vocavit auctoritas, inde scilicet quod divisionem propositionis terminent; ne videlicet ipsa vel ad syllabas vel ad litteras porrigatur, quae non ut partes propositionum accipiendae sunt, cum videlicet significationem per se non impleant, sed magis dictionum. Sed fortasse dicitur Boethius non alios terminos categoricis enuntiationibus assignare quam praedicatum et subiectum' (*Dialectica*, p. 161).

[31] 'Ex his dictis etiam patet, quod haec est imperfecta, *si Socrates currit*, quia ista coniunctio, *si*, huic constructioni addita, *Socrates currit*, facit in ea novam dependentiam ad aliquid extra se, ut ad aliquid consequens, quod si non exprimatur, semper imperfecta manebit, ut dicendo *me legere*: haec est imperfecta, quia animum auditoris non quietat; et si quae sunt similes,' *Grammatica speculativa*, p. 316. *Si quae* is probably a scribe's error for *reliquae*.

[32] 'Et dicunt quidam quod principia perfectionis sunt ista, scilicet suppositum et appositum, et quod suppositum sit per se stans et fixum [i.e., substantive, not adjective], et quod appositum sit modi finiti . . . Et illi qui sic dicunt, supponunt quod perfectio non praesupponat congruitatem, quia omnia illa principia reperiuntur in figurativa constructione . . . Et isti etiam plus dicunt. Dicunt enim quod figurativa constructio plus est congrua et perfecta quam non figurativa . . . quia magis movet intellectum . . . Sed isti non videntur dicere sufficienter, quia si dicatur *Catonis est*, hic sunt omnia principia quae ipsi ponunt esse principia perfectionis . . . sed ista *Catonis est* nec vera nec falsa est, ergo non est perfecta nec indicativa,' pp. 112–13.

[33] Not even Petrus Croccus, as far as I can determine; his section on *figurae* consists mostly of simple definitions of terms. It is possible that he grapples with this issue somewhere else in his voluminous work.

[34] 'Intellectus secundarius . . . resultat ex significatis partium quae sunt sub diversis modis significandi,' p. 20.

[35] The only exception is rotation, which has no endpoints and is therefore, as Aristotle argues, the only kind of motion that can continue eternally; this is why pre-Keplerian astronomers thought it necessary to conceive of celestial motions in terms of rotating spheres.

[36] See Aristotle, *Physics* III (especially 200 b 12 – 201 b 15, 205 a 6–7), VIII.7 (261 a

27–261 b 27) et passim. For the Latin terminology, see for instance Thomas Aquinas' commentary on the *Physics*, e.g., the following: 'Motus est actus mobilis … ex quo apparet quod ad hoc quod est motus, necesse est existere res quae possunt moveri' (book VIII, lectio 2, section 2, p. 367); 'Necesse est quod motui contrarietur … quies quae est in termino a quo' (V, 9, 5, p. 260); 'Motus circularis … non corrumpitur cum venit ad terminum, cum sit idem eius principium et finis' (VIII, 19, 6, p. 439). A look at the entries for these terms in the *Index Thomisticus* illustrates the pervasive influence of Aristotle's *Physics* on scholastic philosophy.

[37] The interpolation of *non* in the last sentence of the first paragraph is my own; it seems to be required by the sense.

[38] These are my own examples; Jordanus gives none.

[39] More eloquently, 'tu es principium misericordiae ex causa quae est in te,' p. 44.

[40] See for example Thomas of Erfurt, *Grammatica speculativa*, pp. 190–2; Radulphus Brito, *Quaestiones* II.3; Simon Dacus Modista, *Quaestiones*, pp. 116–18; and Simon's commentary on Martin, quoted by Enders and Pinborg (1980:358).

[41] John of Genoa, *Catholicon*, section 'De constructione'. (I used the Bodleian Library's copy of the 1490 Venice edition, which lacks page or folio numbers.)

[42] My examples.

[43] 'Dubitatur autem quo accidente debet fieri constructio intransitiva ex parte post. Apparebit quod ratione personae sicut ex parte ante. Motus enim comparatur ad duas extremitates, ad unam a qua est motus ut ad agentem, ad reliquam vero ut ad quam. Si ergo motus ratione illius extremitatis ut a qua est construatur ratione personae, similiter videtur et quod non tantum agit substantia sed etiam patitur quod ratione substantiae debet construi cum termino in quem. Quare videtur quod personalis constructio necessaria sit ad uniendum verbum cum casuali ex parte post sicut ex parte ante. Videtur etiam idem sicut dicit Aristoteles [*Physics* III.3, 202 a 13–14]: motus non est in agente sicut in subiecto sed in patiente. Ergo cum casuale recipiat motum sicut subiectum motus, necessarie magis videatur quod ratione substantiae debeat uniri verbum cum recipiente motum quam cum agente.' (Composite reading based on Vatican ms., fol. 95ra–b, with the corresponding passage in the Munich manuscript.)

[44] 'Numeratur enim motus tripliciter sicut patet per Aristotelem: aut numeratur a numero subiecti in quo est, aut secundum tempus, aut numeratur motus secundum speciem ad quam est motus, sicut dealbatio et denigratio sunt motus specierum. Nullam autem differentiam constructionis recipit verbum a numero temporis, ergo nullam recipiet a numero subiecti …

Ad aliud dicendum quod non est simile de numero temporis et de numero subiecti. Numerus enim temporis verbo non accidit sicut numerus qui est ex parte subiecti. Propter hoc non est constructio verbi ad aliquid secundum illum numerum. Hoc autem patet quod si substantia sit infinita quae in verbo intelligitur, necesse est numerum esse infinitum, hoc autem non esset nisi numerus adveniret ex parte substantiae. Propter hoc dicendum quod verbum recipit differentiam constructionis ex parte numeri quam recipit a substantia, non autem ex parte quam recipit a tempore,' Vatican ms., fol. 94va–b. *Infinitus* here almost certainly means 'unspecified', not 'infinite'.

[45] 'Ad oppositum, in naturalibus [motibus] ita est quod terminus motus a quo potest fieri terminus motus ad quem, ut ab Athenis ad Thebas et e contrario,' pp. 34–5. The example reappears in various places in his treatise.

5: Modistic treatments of particular syntactic problems

[1] 'Omne quod construitur cum alio, requirit in eo modum significandi determinatum, quod apparet in partibus declinabilibus. Nomen enim nominativi casus singularis numeri personae tertiae, cum construatur cum verbo, requirit in eo numerum consimilem ratione numeri sui, et per personam suam consimilem personam, et per casum consimilem casum ... Coniunctio autem in dictionibus inter quas coniungit et disiungit non requirit aliquos modos determinatos significandi, quod probatur, quia potest coniungere inter dictiones diversorum modorum, diversarum personarum et sic de aliis. Ergo et cetera ...

Praeterea: Omnis constructio redditur incongrua ex altero modo significandi vel utroque mutato in aliis modis significandi. Sed si dicatur "homo et asinus", homine et asino mutatis in casibus, numeris et generibus, nulla fit incongruitas; sicut enim bene dicitur "homo et asinus", sic "hominem et asinum", "homines et asinos" et sic de aliis accidentibus. Ergo coniunctio, quamquam in oratione ponatur, tamen non est pars orationis constructibilis,' pp. 302–3.

[2] 'Coniunctio conditionalis in oratione conditionali ordinatur cum toto antecedente, ut "si Socrates currit, Socrates movetur". Sed cum ipso toto antecedente non construitur, quod probatur, quia omnis constructio fit ratione modorum significandi ... Modi enim significandi sunt dictionum et non orationum,' p. 303.

[3] 'Omnis constructio aut est transitiva aut intransitiva. Coniunctio autem non habet constructionem transitivam nec intransitivam, sive fiat transitio actuum sive personarum, ut de se patet, ergo et cetera,' p. 304.

[4] William of Sherwood (Shirwood, Shyreswoode), *Syncategoremata*, ed. O'Donnell, p. 48. His entire list of syncategorematic terms includes: *omnis, totum, uterque, nullus, nihil, neutrum, praeter, solus, tantum, est, non, necessario, contingenter, incipit, desinit, si, nisi, quin, et, vel, ne, sive*. This is apparently not meant to be exhaustive; it omits, for example, *aut*.

[5] 'Solet dici quod sicut constructibilia quae sunt unita per coniunctionem construuntur, ita et coniunctio construitur. Unde dicendo "Socrates et Plato currunt" hoc quod est "et" habet constructionem intransitivam sicut constructibilia inter quae coniungit, et dicendo "video Socratem et Platonem" hoc quod est "et" habet constructionem transitivam,' *Quaestiones* I. 24, pp. 176–7. The proponents of this position apparently want to draw a third arrow, from the verb to the conjunction, and are assuming that the first two arrows are, so to speak, already there.

[6] 'Dicendo "Socrates et Plato" hic coniunctio habet constructionem cum extremis et quoad illam speciem construendi non eget alio constructibili,' p. 177.

[7] Thomas of Erfurt gives what may be a hint – but only a hint – of a way to get out of this problem: he remarks that the conjunction 'links the subject to the predicate' ('coniungit suppositum apposito,' *Grammatica speculativa*, p. 294). This suggests that he may have viewed the conjunction as a *medium construendi* rather than as the

endpoint of a *constructio* (compare Jordanus, pp. 49–50), and hence that on his analysis the plural feature could in some sense be ascribed to *et* without making *et* the subject of the sentence. However, his remarks are too brief for this to be inferred with certainty.

[8] Or perhaps because it signifies a chronologically earlier event. In either case, the argument is not particularly to the point.

[9] This gives the analysis proposed by Norimbergensis an advantage over that proposed by Siger de Courtrai (*sophisma* 'Magistro legente pueri proficiunt', p. 54), in which one whole clause governs the other.

[10] Except, perhaps, the transubstantiated Eucharist. The relevant metaphysical ground had been plowed over thoroughly in connection with the Eucharistic controversies of the eleventh and twelfth centuries, but to explore it here would take us far afield.

[11] 'Et tu diceres, "modus significandi accidentalis praesupponit essentialem; si ergo oratio habebit modum accidentalem, habebit etiam essentialem, et sic redit idem quod prius." Ista instantia ⟨est⟩ soluta in quaestionibus primi libri. Nam ut ibi visum est maior potest negari, quia modi significandi non respiciunt se ordine prioris et posterioris ut absolute sumuntur, sicut neque rei proprietates a quibus sumuntur. Vel si volumus, maior concedi potest; non tamen oportet propter hoc quod habeat modum essentialem per se et primo, sed sufficit quod habeat in suis partibus,' Anonymus Norimbergensis, fol. 51ra; cf. Radulphus Brito, pp. 333–4.

[12] 'Sed diceres, immo tales ablativi [i.e., the ablative absolute] faciunt orationem perfectam, quia ... illa "magistro legente" exponitur per istam "dum magister legit", et ista est perfecta, cum habeat suppositum et appositum quae ad constructionis perfectionem requiruntur ... Dicendum quod ratio illa non valet, quia ... ista "dum magister legit" non est perfecta, immo ratione adverbii est: quamvis "dum" superaddati dependentiam habet ad consequens quod not exprimatur supra, imperfecta est,' fol. 51ra.

[13] '"Semper antecedit" et cetera verum est quanto ad actualem prolationem, sed non quanto ad naturalem construendi ordinem,' ibid. He is replying, of course, to the passage 'Item si ablativi ... ' quoted above.

[14] 'Tunc ad dictum Petri Heliae et aliorum: potest dici quod loquuntur secundum usum, non secundum artem, nam secundum usum communiter loquentium, illi ablativi dicuntur poni absolute non a constructione vel regimine, sed quia carent requisita et determinata ordinatione,' ibid.

[15] See, for example, Pseudo-Albertus, Questions 19–20; Simon Dacus Modista, *Quaestiones*, pp. 151–8 and 162–70; and Boethius Dacus, Questions 90–4.

[16] 'Quaeritur utrum verba impersonalia passivae vocis ab activis [sc. transitivis] descendentia construantur cum accusativo a parte post ut dicendo "legitur Vergilium", includendo cum hoc utrum simul et semel possint construi, non repetita eadem voce' (p. 314).

[17] 'Omne verbum requirit suppositum, cuius ratio est quia eadem est comparatio verbi ad suppositum quae est accidentis concreti ad subiectum. Sed omne accidens concretum praeexigit subiectum cui insit, ideo omne verbum praeexigit suppositum' (p. 322).

An *accidens concretum* is one that is in no sense conceived of as an entity in itself; for instance, 'white' and 'just' refer to concrete accidents, while 'whiteness' and 'justice' refer to abstract accidents. See Ockham, *Summa logicae* I.5.

[18] 'Haec positio non valet quia sic possemus omni verbo dare suppositum, cum in omni verbi intelligatur nominativus suae rei, ut in "curro" cursus et sic de aliis' (p. 323).

[19] 'Accusativus videtur ibi significare in ratione principii respectu actus et genitivus magis in ratione termini' (p. 323).

[20] 'Et huiusmodi est evidentissimum signum, quia sua participia retinent constructionem cum genitivo dicendo "paenitens peccati", "pudens vitii" et non cum accusativo. Participia autem tantum retinent constructionem suorum verborum post se ad obliquum, non eam quam habent ante se ad suppositum ... Cum ergo participia istorum verborum tantum retineant constructionem cum genitivo, patet quod sua verba requirunt genitivum post se transitive et non accusativum' (p. 323).

Although phrased in the flowing style of the original, this passage is attested only as a marginal addition to the Nuremberg manuscript and may not be original.

[21] '(Suppositio) est simplex quando dictio supponit significatum pro significato, ut "homo est species", personalis autem quando supponit significatum, sed pro re quae subest, ut "homo currit"' (William of Sherwood, *Introductiones*, p. 75). For twelfth-century statements of essentially the same doctrine, see de Rijk (1967a : 588–9); for a handy summary, Pinborg (1972 : 61–5).

Naturally, there was plenty of room for controversy over the nature of the universal thing that a word in *suppositio simplex* stands for. De Rijk's sources identify it with a Platonic-sounding *forma universalis*, while Ockham is at pains to explain that it is nothing more than a concept in the speaker's mind (*Summa logicae* I.64, p. 196).

[22] As noted by Thurot (1868 : 355–72), and explored in depth by Kneepkens (1976, 1977), whom I follow closely in this section.

[23] Lines 1449–50 of the *Doctrinale* read as follows:

> Occurretque tibi quandoque relatio simplex:
> 'Femina, quae clausit vitae portam, reseravit.'

For long extracts from Robert Blund see Kneepkens (1977).

[24] 'Item illa constructibilia quae ad invicem construuntur debent proportionari in modis significandi. Sed relativum et antecedens non conformantur in modis significandi, ergo et cetera. Maior patet; probatio minoris, quia relativum et antecedens non conformantur in casu aliquando quia bene dicitur "Socrates currit quem video, cuius misereor, cui indulgeo" et sic de aliis ... Nec etiam oportet conformari in genere quia bene dicitur "ex semine tuo qui est Christus" ... nec oportet proportionari in numero et persona ut patet de persona "ego sum qui sum", de numero "Deus creavit hominem, masculum et feminam creavit eos"' (p. 243).

[25] Part of this passage was quoted in section 4.5 (on *primum* and *secundum*) above. At that point I had not introduced the term 'anaphor' in its medieval sense, so I translated *relativum* as 'relative'.

6: Subsequent developments

[1] Here I rely heavily on the account given by Pinborg (1967, especially pp. 167–212; 1975b; and 1982).

[2] The first item in the first of the many paradigms in Donatus' *Ars minor* (*Ars grammatica*, pp. 355–6).

[3] The two passages quoted occur in the opposite order in the original.

[4] The *Destructiones* are quoted extensively by Pinborg (1967:204–7); see also Ludger Kaczmarek's newly released edition, *Modi significandi und ihre Destruktionen: zwei Texte zur scholastischen Sprachtheorie in 14. Jahrhundert* (Materialien zur Geschichte der Sprachwissenschaft und der Semiotik, 1. Münster: Münsteraner Arbeitskreis für Semiotik, 1980).

D'Ailly (Petrus de Alliaco) was an interesting character in a number of respects. He is noted mostly for his pointed invectives against corruption in the Church; in addition, he produced a number of astronomical and geographical works, including the book (*Imago mundi*) that is said to have given Christopher Columbus the idea that he could get to Asia by sailing west.

[5] To take an example from Despauterius (1537:186):

Syntaxi sive constructioni quot accidunt? Duo, Concordantia et Regimen. Concordantia quid est? Debita partium orationis convenientia in genere, numero, casu vel persona.

He does not find it necessary to define *regimen*.

[6] The title page gives the title as *Praeclara Donati expositio secundum viam Nominalium, enucleans de partibus orationis quaestiones*; it is the colophon that labels it *Expositio Donati nominalis*.

[7] The author quotes Priscian's definition of the noun rather loosely from *Institutiones* II.22. I have not been able to identify the 'author of the Modes of Signifying' that he refers to; it was more usual to say that the noun signifies *per modum habitus et quietis* (Martin of Dacia, p. 10) or *per modum esse* (Thomas of Erfurt, p. 152). Radulphus Brito does use the *modus substantiae* definition (*Quaestiones* I.29, pp. 192–3), but his *Quaestiones* were not widely used as a standard handbook. In any case, Boethius Dacus makes a point of explaining that *modus habitus* and *modus substantiae* are equivalent (p. 101).

[8] 'Modi vero essentiales sunt qui exprimuntur per terminos positos in definitionibus essentialibus partium,' fol. 3vb.

[9] Despauterius (1537:228–9); Hugh of St Victor, *De grammatica*, pp. 108–9 (cited in section 2.3 above).

Bibliography

Works that originated before the invention of printing are listed as 'Ancient and medieval sources' and cited by author's name, title (where more than one work by a given author is listed), and traditional sectionation or, if there is none, page number in the edition listed here. Works originally issued in printed form, no matter how early, are treated as modern sources and cited by author, date, and page.

Ancient and medieval sources

Abelard (Abailard), Peter (1079–1142). *Dialectica*, ed. L. M. de Rijk. 2nd edn. (Philosophical Texts and Studies, 1.) Assen, Holland: Van Gorcum, 1970.

Albertus Magnus, Pseudo- (c. 1285). *Quaestiones Alberti de modis significandi*, ed. and trans. L. G. Kelly. (Amsterdam Studies in the Theory and History of Linguistic Science, III: Studies in the History of Linguistics, 15.) Amsterdam: John Benjamins, 1977.

Albertus Swebelinus (c. 1290/1300). Commentary on the *Modi significandi* of Martin of Dacia. Unedited manuscript. St Florian: Stiftsbibliothek, XI:264, fols. 189r–213v.

Alcuin of York (fl. 781–96). *Grammatica*. In his *Opera quae hactenus reperiri possunt*, ed. Andreas Quercetanus, vol. I, pp. 1255–1319. Paris: Sebastianus Cramoisy, 1617.

Alexander de Villa Dei (Alexandre de Villedieu) (1199?). *Doctrinale*. Critical edition with introduction by Dietrich Reichling. (Monumenta Germaniae paedagogica, 12.) Berlin: A. Hofmann, 1893.

Alfarabi (870–950). *Catálogo de las ciencias* [*Liber de scientiis*], ed. and trans. Ángel González Palencia. (Publicaciones de la Facultad de Filosofía y Letras, Universidad de Madrid, 2.) Madrid: Estanislao Maestre, 1932.

Algazel (al-Ghazzālī) (1058/9–1111). *Algazel's Metaphysics: A Medieval Translation*, ed. J. T. Muckle, CSB. Toronto: St Michael's College, 1933.

Anonymous (before 1500). *Expositio Donati nominalis* [or] *Praeclara Donati expositio secundum viam Nominalium enucleans de partibus orationis quaestiones*. Rouen: Laurentius Hostingue and Jametus Louys for Robert Mace, 1500.

Anonymus Cracoviensis (c. 1300). Questions on *Priscianus minor*. Unedited manuscript. Cracow: Biblioteka Jagiellońska, 649, fols. 231r–252v.

Anonymus Norimbergensis (c. 1300). Questions on *Priscianus minor*. Manuscript, partially edited by Pinborg (1980b). Nürnberg: Stadtbibliothek, Cent.V.21, fols. 30r–53r.

Apollonius Dyscolus (c. 125). *Apollonii Dyscoli quae supersunt*, ed. Richardus Schneider and Gustavus Uhlig. (Grammatici Graeci, part II, vols. 1–3.) Leipzig: Teubner, 1878–1910.

Aquinas. *See* Thomas Aquinas.

Aristotle (384–322 BC). *The Categories; On Interpretation* [*De interpretatione*, Περὶ Ἑρμηνείας], ed. and trans. Harold P. Cook; *Prior Analytics*, ed. and trans. Hugh Tredennick. (Loeb Classical Library.) London: Heinemann; Cambridge, Massachusetts: Harvard University Press, 1938.

Metaphysics, ed. and trans. Hugh Tredennick. 2 vols. (Loeb Classical Library.) London: Heinemann; Cambridge, Massachusetts: Harvard University Press, 1933–5.

Physics, ed. and trans. Philip H. Wicksteed and Francis M. Cornford. 2 vols. (Loeb Classical Library.) Cambridge, Massachusetts: Harvard University Press, 1957–60.

Posterior Analytics, ed. and trans. Hugh Tredennick. (Loeb Classical Library.) London: Heinemann; Cambridge, Massachusetts: Harvard University Press, 1938.

On Sophistical Refutations [*Sophistici elenchi*] and *On Coming-To-Be and Passing-Away* [*De generatione et corruptione*], ed. and trans. E. S. Forster. (Loeb Classical Library.) London: Heinemann; Cambridge, Massachusetts: Harvard University Press, 1955.

Bacon, Roger (1214?–94). *The Greek Grammar of Roger Bacon and a Fragment of his Hebrew Grammar*, ed. Edmond Nolan and S. A. Hirsch. Cambridge University Press, 1902.

(c. 1240). *Summa grammatica*, ed. Robert Steele. (*Opera hactenus inedita Rogeri Baconi*, 15.) Oxford: Clarendon Press, 1940.

Boethius, Anicius Manlius Severinus (480–525 AD). *Commentarii in librum Aristotelis 'Peri hermeneias'*, ed. Carolus Meiser. 2 vols. Leipzig: Teubner, 1876, 1880.

Liber de divisione. Patrologiae cursus completus, series latina, ed. J.-P. Migne, vol. 64, cols. 875–910. Paris, 1847.

Boethius Dacus (c. 1270). *Modi significandi, sive Quaestiones super Priscianum maiorem*, ed. Jan Pinborg and Heinrich Roos. (Corpus philosophorum Danicorum medii aevi, IV.) Copenhagen: G. E. C. Gad, 1969.

Donatus, Aelius (c. 350). *Ars grammatica* (including *Ars minor*), ed. Henricus Keil. (Grammatici Latini, ed. Henricus Keil, vol. 4, 353–402.) Leipzig: Teubner, 1864. Reprint, Hildesheim: Georg Olms, 1961.

Eberhardus Bethuniensis (1212?). *Graecismus*, ed. Iohannes Wrobel. Breslau: Koebner, 1887.

Goswin of Marbais (Gosvinus de Marbasio, c. 1260). Tractatus de constructione. Unedited manuscript. Paris: Bibliothèque Nationale, fonds latin, 15135, fols. 72–84.

Grosseteste, Robertus de (Pseudo-) (c. 1250). '*Tractatus de grammatica*': eine *fälschlich Robert Grosseteste zugeschriebene spekulative Grammatik*, edited with a commentary by Karl Reichl. (Veröffentlichungen des Grabmann-Institutes, neue Folge, 28.) Munich: Ferdinand Schöningh, 1976.

Gundissalinus, Dominicus (Domingo Gundisalvo) (mid 1100s). *De divisione philosophiae*, ed. Ludwig Baur. (Beiträge zur Geschichte der Philosophie des Mittelalters, 4.2–3.) Münster: Aschendorff, 1903.

Hugh of St Victor (1096/7–1141). *De grammatica. Hugonis de Sancto Victore opera propaedeutica*, ed. Roger Baron, pp. 67–166. (University of Notre Dame Publications in Medieval Studies, 20.) Notre Dame, Indiana: University of Notre Dame Press, 1966.

Johannes Balbus de Janua. See John of Genoa.

Johannes Dacus (1280). *Opera*, ed. Alfred Otto. 2 vols. (Corpus philosophorum Danicorum medii aevi, I.1–2.) Copenhagen: G. E. C. Gad, 1955.

Johannes Josse. *See* Josse de Marvilla, Johannes.

Johannes le Rus (c. 1230/50). *Summa magistri Iohannis le Rus de arte grammatica.* Unedited manuscripts. Rome: Vatican Library, ms. Vat. Lat. 7678, fols. 89r–101v; London: British Library, Additional Manuscript 8167, fols. 136r–154r; Munich: Staatsbibliothek, CLM 7205, fols. 59r–67r.

John of Genoa (Johannes Balbus de Janua) (d. 1298?). *Catholicon.* Venice, 1490. (This is one of many early printed editions.)

Jordanus (of Saxony [?]) (d. 1237). *Notulae super Priscianum minorem magistri Jordani*, partial edition and introduction by Mary Sirridge. (*Cahiers de l'Institut du Moyen Age Grec et Latin*, 36.) University of Copenhagen, 1980.

Josse de Marvilla, Johannes (1322). *Expositiones modorum significandi* [*Tractatus metricus de modis significandi*]. Edition containing an anonymous commentary (inc.: 'Iste est tractatus de modis significandi quem magister Iohannes Iosse de Marvilla Lothoringus ad utilitatem iuvenum composuit ... '). Rouen: Robert Mace, no date (c. 1500).

Kilwardby, Robert (c. 1250). *De ortu scientiarum*, ed. Albert G. Judy. (Auctores Britannici medii aevi, 4.) London: British Academy, 1976.

Kilwardby, Robert (Pseudo-) (c. 1250). *The Commentary on 'Priscianus Maior' Ascribed to Robert Kilwardby*, ed. K. M. Fredborg, N. J. Green-Pedersen, Lauge Nielsen, and Jan Pinborg, with introductory matter by Jan Pinborg and Osmund Lewry, OP. (Cahiers de l'Institut du Moyen Age Grec et Latin, 15.) University of Copenhagen, 1975.

Martin of Dacia (Martinus de Dacia) (c. 1270). *Modi significandi.* In his *Opera*, ed. H. Roos, pp. 1–118. (Corpus philosophorum Danicorum medii aevi, II.) Copenhagen: G. E. C. Gad, 1961.

Michael of Marbais (?) (Michael de Marbasio) (Michel de Marbais) (c. 1285). [In] minus volumen Prisciani. Unedited manuscript. Brussels: Bibliothèque Royale, 10893–4, fols. 63r–126v.

Norimbergensis. *See* Anonymus Norimbergensis.

Ockham (Occam), William of (1323?). *Summa logicae*, ed. Philotheus Boehner, OFM, Gedeon Gál, OFM, and Stephanus Brown. (Guillielmi de Ockham opera philosophica, 1.) St Bonaventure, New York: Franciscan Institute Publications, 1974.

Petrus Croccus (Petrus de Crocco) (c. 1275). Commentary on the *Doctrinale* of Alexander de Villa Dei. Unedited manuscript. Troyes: Bibliothèque de Troyes (Bibliothèque Municipale), 1142, fols. 77r–126v.

Petrus Helias (c. 1140). *The Summa of Petrus Helias on Priscianus Minor*, ed. James E. Tolson, with introduction by Margaret Gibson. (Cahiers de l'Institut du Moyen Age Grec et Latin, 27 and 28.) University of Copenhagen, 1978.

Petrus Hispanus (Pope John XXI) (c. 1205–77). *Tractatus, called afterward Summulae Logicales*, ed. L. M. de Rijk. (Philosophical Texts and Studies, 22.) Assen, Holland: Van Gorcum, 1972.

Priscianus Caesariensis (c. 500). *Institutionum grammaticarum libri XVIII*, ed. Martinus Hertz. (Grammatici Latini, ed. Henricus Keil, 2 and 3.) Leipzig: Teubner, 1855, 1859. Reprint, Hildesheim: Georg Olms, 1961.

Radulphus Brito (Raoul le Breton) (Rodolphe le Breton) (c. 1300). *Quaestiones super Priscianum minorem*, ed. Heinz W. Enders and Jan Pinborg. 2 vols. (Grammatica speculativa, 3.) Stuttgart–Bad Cannstatt: Frommann-Holzboog, 1980.

Remigius of Auxerre (c. 900). *Remigii Autissodorensis in artem Donati minorem commentum*, ed. W. Fox, SJ. Leipzig: Teubner, 1902.

Sedulius Scottus (fl. 848–58). *Commentum Sedulii Scotti in maiorem Donatum grammaticum*, ed. Denis G. Brearley. Toronto: Pontifical Institute of Medieval Studies, 1975.

Sherwood (Shirwood, Shyreswoode). *See* William of Sherwood.

Siger de Courtrai (Sigerus de Cortraco) (c. 1320). *Summa modorum significandi; sophismata*, ed. Jan Pinborg. (Amsterdam Studies in the Theory and History of Linguistic Science, III: Studies in the History of Linguistics, 14.) Amsterdam: Benjamins.

Simon Dacus Domifex. *Domus grammaticae* (c. 1250/70). In Otto 1963: 1–88.

Simon Dacus Modista (c. 1285/90). *Quaestiones super secundum minoris voluminis Prisciani*. In Otto 1963: 89–178.

(?). Commentary on the *Modi significandi* of Martin of Dacia (Rhetoricae primo scribit philosophus 'Turpe est ignorare ... '). Unedited manuscripts. Brugge: Staadsbiblioteek, 535, fols. 64–96; Klagenfurt: Studienbibliothek, Perg. 13, fols. 66–108; Leipzig: Karl-Marx-Universität, Universitätsbibliothek, 1356, fols. 29–45.

Sponcius Provincialis (Sponcius le Provençal) (1242). *De constructione*. Ed. in Fierville 1886: 177–92.

Stoicorum veterum fragmenta, ed. Iohannes ab Arnim. 4 vols. Leipzig: Teubner, 1903–24.

Thomas Aquinas (1225–74). *Commentaria in octo libros Physicorum Aristotelis. Sancti Thomae Aquinatis opera*, edited by the Dominican Order (Leonine edition), vol. 2. Rome: Vatican Polyglot Press, 1874.

In quatuor libros Sententiarum. Sancti Thomae Aquinatis opera omnia ut sunt in Indice Thomistico, edited (with text taken from the 1856–8 Parma edition) by Robertus Busa, SJ, vol. 1. Stuttgart–Bad Cannstatt: Frommann-Holzboog, 1980.

Thomas of Erfurt (Thomasius de Erfordia) (c. 1300). *Grammatica speculativa* [original title, *Novi modi significandi*], edited with translation and commentary by G. L. Bursill-Hall. (The Classics of Linguistics.) London: Longman, 1972. (All citations of Thomas of Erfurt refer to this edition unless otherwise noted. In quoting from this work I have used my own English translations, rather than Bursill-Hall's, in order to achieve greater consistency in translating technical terminology.)

Fundamentum puerorum. Ed. in Gansiniec 1960:105–6.

Modi significandi [= *Grammatica speculativa*]. (Colophon: Finit liber modorum significandi Alberti.) Deventer: Richardus Pafroed, 1489.

Thomas de Hancya (Haneya?) (1313). Tractatus de quattuor partibus grammaticae (Memoriale iuniorum). Unedited manuscript. Oxford: Bodleian Library, ms. Bodley 643, fols. 127–255.

Vincent of Beauvais (Vincentius Bellovacensis) (fl. 1244–64). *Speculum doctrinale.* In his *Bibliotheca mundi,* edited by the Benedictine monks at Douai, vol. 4. Douai, 1624. Reprint, Graz: Akademische Druck- und Verlaganstalt, 1964–5.

William of Conches (Guillaume de Conches) (c. 1080–c. 1154). *De philosophia mundi libri quatuor.* (Attributed to Honorius Augustodunensis.) *Patrologiae cursus completus, series latina,* ed. J.-P. Migne, vol. 172, cols. 39–102. Paris, 1854.

William of Ockham. *See* Ockham.

William of Sherwood (Shirwood, Shyreswoode) (c. 1260). 'Die *Introductiones in logicam* des Wilhelm von Shyreswood († nach 1267): literarhistorische Einleitung und Textausgabe,' by Martin Grabmann. *Sitzungsberichte der Bayerischen Akademie der Wissenschaften, Philosophisch–historische Abteilung,* 1937, part 10.

Syncategoremata, ed. J. Reginald O'Donnell, OSB. *Medieval Studies* 3:46–93.

Modern sources

Andrés, Teodoro de, SJ. 1969. *El nominalismo de Guillermo de Ockham como filosofía del lenguaje.* Madrid: Editorial Gredos, SA.

Bauer, Laurie. 1979. Some thoughts on dependency grammar. *Linguistics* 17 (new numbering) 301–15.

Baum, Richard. 1976. *'Dependenzgrammatik': Tesnières Modell der Sprachbeschreibung in wissenschaftsgeschichtlicher und kritischer Sicht.* (Zeitschrift für romanische Philologie, supplement 151.) Tübingen: Max Niemeyer.

Bloomfield, Leonard. 1933. *Language.* New York: Holt, Reinhart & Winston.

Bursill-Hall, G. L. 1963. Mediaeval grammatical theories. *Canadian Journal of Linguistics* 9:39–54.

1966. Aspects of modistic grammar. *Georgetown University Monograph Series on Languages and Linguistics* 19:133–48.

1971. *Speculative Grammars of the Middle Ages: The Doctrine of Partes Orationis of the Modistae.* The Hague: Mouton.

1972. = his edition of Thomas of Erfurt, q.v.

1981. *A Census of Medieval Latin Grammatical Manuscripts.* (Grammatica speculativa, 4.) Stuttgart–Bad Cannstatt: Frommann-Holzboog.

Cambridge History of Later Medieval Philosophy, The. = Kretzmann, Kenny, and Pinborg 1982, q.v.

Carden, Guy. 1973. *English Quantifiers: Logical Structure and Linguistic Variation.* Tokyo: Taishukan.

Covington, Michael A. 1979. The syntactic theory of Thomas of Erfurt. *Linguistics* 17 (new numbering) 465–96.

Despauterius, Johannes. 1537. *Commentarii grammatici.* Paris: Robert Étienne.

Ebbesen, S. 1981. Early supposition-theory (12th–13th centuries). *Histoire, épistémologie, langage* 3 : 35–48.

Enders, Heinz W., and Pinborg, Jan. 1980. = their edition of Radulphus Brito, q.v.

Fierville, Charles. 1886. *Une grammaire latine inédite du XIIIe siècle, extraite des manuscrits No. 465 de Laon et No. 15462 (fonds latin) de la Bibliothèque Nationale.* Paris: Imprimerie Nationale.

Fredborg, Karin Margareta. 1973. The dependence of Petrus Helias' *Summa super Priscianum* on William of Conches's *Glose super Priscianum. Cahiers de l'Institut du Moyen Age Grec et Latin* 11 : 1–57. University of Copenhagen.

1980. Universal grammar according to some twelfth-century grammarians. *Historiographia Linguistica* 7 : 69–84.

1981. Some notes on the grammar of William of Conches. *Cahiers de l'Institut du Moyen Age Grec et Latin* 37 : 21–41. University of Copenhagen.

Gansiniec, Ryszard. 1960. *Metrificale Marka z Opatowca i traktaty gramatyczne XIV i XV wieku.* (Studia Staropolskie, VI.) Wrocław: Zakład Norodowy im. Ossolinskich.

Grabmann, Martin. 1940. *Die Sophismataliteratur des 12. und 13. Jahrhunderts mit Textausgabe eines Sophisma des Boetius von Dacien.* (Beiträge zur Geschichte der Philosophie und Theologie des Mittelalters, 36.1.) Münster: Aschendorff.

Hockett, Charles F. 1954. Two models of grammatical description. *Word* 10 : 210–31. Reprinted in *Readings in Linguistics*, I, ed. Martin Joos. 4th ed. University of Chicago Press, 1966, 386–99.

Hudson, Richard A. 1980. Constituency and dependency. *Linguistics* 18 (new numbering) 179–98.

Hunt, R. W. 1943. Studies on Priscian in the eleventh and twelfth centuries, I: Petrus Helias and his predecessors. *Medieval and Renaissance Studies* 1 : 194–231. Reprinted in Hunt 1980 : 1–38.

1950. Studies on Priscian in the eleventh and twelfth centuries, II: The school of Ralph of Beauvais. *Medieval and Renaissance Studies* 2 : 1–56. Reprinted in Hunt 1980 : 39–94.

1980. *The History of Grammar in the Middle Ages: Collected Papers*, ed. G. L. Bursill-Hall. (Amsterdam Studies in the Theory and History of Linguistic Science, III: Studies in the History of Linguistics, 5.) Amsterdam: Benjamins. (Articles reprinted in this volume are cited by the original page numbers, which are shown in the reprinted edition.)

Jeauneau, Édouard. 1960. Deux rédactions des gloses de Guillaume de Conches sur Priscien. *Recherches de théologie ancienne et médiévale* 27 : 212–47. Reprinted in his *Lectio philosophorum: recherches sur l'école de Chartres* (Amsterdam: Hakkert, 1973), 335–70.

Kelly, L. G. 1977a. La *Physique* d'Aristote et la phrase simple dans les ouvrages de grammaire spéculative. *La grammaire générale: des modistes aux idéologues*, ed. André Joly and Jean Stéfanini, pp. 107–24. Villeneuve d'Ascq: Publications de l'Université de Lille III.

1977b. = his edition of Pseudo-Albertus Magnus, q.v.

1979. *Modus significandi*: an interdisciplinary concept. *Historiographia Linguistica* 6: 159–80.

Kneale, William, and Kneale, Martha. 1962. *The Development of Logic*. Oxford: Clarendon Press.

Kneepkens, C. H. 1976. *Mulier quae damnavit salvavit*: a note on the early development of the *relatio simplex*. *Vivarium* 14: 1–25.

1977. The *relatio simplex* in the grammatical tracts of the late twelfth and early thirteenth century. *Vivarium* 15: 1–30.

1978. Magister Guido's view on government: On twelfth century linguistic thought. *Vivarium* 16: 108–41.

Kretzmann, Norman; Kenny, Anthony; and Pinborg, Jan, eds. 1982. *The Cambridge History of Later Medieval Philosophy*. Cambridge University Press.

Lewis, C. S. 1964. *The Discarded Image: An Introduction to Medieval and Renaissance Literature*. Cambridge University Press.

Linacre, Thomas. 1524. *De emendata structura latini sermonis libri sex*. London: Richard Pynson. Reprint, Menston (England): Scolar Press, 1968.

Lindberg, David C., ed. 1978. *Science in the Middle Ages*. (Chicago History of Science and Medicine.) University of Chicago Press.

Mahdi, Muhsin. 1975. Science, philosophy, and religion in Alfarabi's *Enumeration of the Sciences*. *The Cultural Context of Medieval Learning: Proceedings of the First International Conference on Philosophy, Science, and Theology in the Middle Ages*, ed. John Emery Murdoch and Edith Dudley Sylla, pp. 113–47. (Synthese Library, 76.) Dordrecht and Boston: D. Reidel.

Matthews, P. H. 1981. *Syntax*. Cambridge University Press.

Murphy, James J. 1974. *Rhetoric in the Middle Ages: A History of Rhetorical Theory from St. Augustine to the Renaissance*. Berkeley, Los Angeles, and London: University of California Press.

Otto, Alfred, ed. 1963. *Simonis Daci opera*. (Corpus philosophorum Danicorum medii aevi, III.) Copenhagen: G. E. C. Gad.

Padley, G. A. 1976. *Grammatical Theory in Western Europe, 1500–1700: The Latin Tradition*. Cambridge University Press.

Paetow, Louis John. 1910. *The Arts Course at Medieval Universities with Special Reference to Grammar and Rhetoric*. (The University Studies, vol. III, no. 7.) Urbana–Champaign: University of Illinois Press.

Parret, Herman, ed. 1976. *History of Linguistic Thought and Contemporary Linguistics*. Berlin and New York: Walter de Gruyter.

Percival, W. Keith. 1975. The grammatical tradition and the rise of the vernaculars. *Current Trends in Linguistics*, ed. Thomas A. Sebeok, vol. 13, pp. 231–75. The Hague: Mouton.

1976. Deep and surface structure concepts in Renaissance and medieval syntactic theory. In Parret 1976:238–54.

(To appear.) Syntax in the Middle Ages.

Pinborg, Jan. 1967. *Die Entwicklung der Sprachtheorie im Mittelalter.* (Beiträge zur Geschichte der Philosophie und Theologie des Mittelalters, 42.2.) Münster: Aschendorff; Copenhagen: Arne Frost-Hansen.

1972. *Logik und Semantik im Mittelalter.* (Problemata, 10.) Stuttgart–Bad Cannstatt: Frommann-Holzboog.

1973. Some syntactical concepts in medieval grammar. *Classica et mediaevalia Francisco Blatt septuagenario dedicata*, ed. O. S. Due et al. (Classica et Mediaevalia, Dissertatio IX), 496–509. Copenhagen: Gyldendal.

1974. Review of Bursill-Hall's edition of Thomas of Erfurt (1972). *Lingua* 34:369–73.

1975a. Die Logik der Modistae. *Studia mediewistyczne* 16:39–97.

1975b. A note on some theoretical concepts of logic and grammar. *Revue internationale de philosophie* 113:286–96.

1979. The English contribution to logic before Ockham. *Synthese* 40:19–42.

1980a. Leben und Werke des Radulphus Brito. In Radulphus Brito, *Quaestiones*, ed. Enders and Pinborg, pp. 13–26.

1980b. Can constructions be construed? A problem in medieval syntactical theory. *Historiographia Linguistica* 7:201–10.

1982. Speculative grammar. *The Cambridge History of Later Medieval Philosophy*, ed. Norman Kretzmann, Anthony Kenny and Jan Pinborg, pp. 254–69. Cambridge University Press.

Ramus, Petrus (Pierre de la Ramée). 1559. *Scholae grammaticae*. Paris: Andreas Wechel.

1580. *Grammatica*. Frankfurt: Andreas Wechel.

Rijk, L. M. de, 1962, 1967a, 1967b. *Logica Modernorum: A Contribution to the History of Early Terminist Logic.* 2 vols., the second volume in two parts. (Philosophical Texts and Studies, 6 and 16.) Assen, Holland: Van Gorcum.

1970. = his edition of Abelard, q.v.

1972. = his edition of Petrus Hispanus, q.v.

Robins, R. H. 1959. In defence of WP. *Transactions of the Philological Society 1959*, 116–44.

1967. *A Short History of Linguistics.* London: Longman; Bloomington: Indiana University Press.

1974. Theory-orientation versus data-orientation; a recurrent theme in linguistics. *Historiographia Linguistica* 1:11–26.

1980. Functional syntax in medieval Europe. *Historiographia Linguistica* 7:231–40.

Roos, Heinrich, SJ. 1952. *Die Modi significandi des Martinus de Dacia.* (Beiträge zur Geschichte der Philosophie und Theologie des Mittelalters, 37.2.) Münster: Aschendorff; Copenhagen: Arne Frost-Hansen.

Rosier, Irène. 1981a. La notion de partie du discours dans la grammaire spéculative. *Histoire, épistémologie, langage* 3:49–62.

1981b. Transitivité et ordre des mots chez les grammairiens médiévaux. Paper read at the Second International Conference on the History of the Language Sciences. Lille. (To be published in conference proceedings.)

(To appear A.) Régime et dépendance chez les grammairiens médiévaux.

(To appear B.) *La grammaire spéculative des modistes.* Lille: Presses Universitaires de Lille.

Sanctius, Franciscus, Brocensis (Francisco Sánchez de las Brozas). 1562. *Minerva, seu de latinae linguae causis et elegantia.* 1st edn. Modern edition with introduction by Eduardo del Estal Fuentes. (Acta Salamanctensia, Filosofía y Letras, 92.) University of Salamanca, 1975.

—— 1587. *Minerva, seu de causis linguae latinae.* Reprinted with annotations by Gaspar Scioppius and Jacobus Perizonius. 7th edn. Amsterdam: P. den Hengst and sons, 1789.

Scaliger, Julius Caesar. 1540. *De causis linguae latinae.* Lyons: S. Gryphius.

Sirridge, Mary. 1980. = her edition of Jordanus, q.v.

Southern, Richard William. 1953. *The Making of the Middle Ages.* New Haven: Yale University Press.

Tesnière, Lucien. 1959. *Éléments de syntaxe structurale.* Paris: Klincksieck.

Thurot, Charles. 1868. *Notices et extraits de divers manuscrits latins pour servir à l'histoire des doctrines grammaticales au moyen âge.* (Notices et extraits des manuscrits de la Bibliothèque Impériale, vol. 22, part 2.) Paris: Imprimerie Impériale.

Tredennick, Hugh. 1938. = his edition of Aristotle's *Posterior Analytics*, q.v.

Vater, Heinz. 1975. Toward a generative dependency grammar. *Lingua* 36:121–45.

Wells, Rulon. 1947. Immediate constituents. *Language* 23:81–117.

Index of names

Abelard, Peter, 9, 11, 16, 144
'Admirantes', 78
Albertus Magnus, Pseudo-, 23, 34, 80,
    138–9, 143, 147
Albertus Swebelinus, 24, 88
Alcuin of York, 4, 8–9
Alexander de Villa Dei (Villedieu), 13,
    130–1
    commentaries on, 23, 47, 50, 78, 135, 140
    relatio simplex, 115, 148
Alfarabi, 19–20, 137
Algazel, 20
Amplonius, 135
Andrés, T. de, 122
Anonymus Cracoviensis, 24
Anonymus Norimbergensis, 24, 47, 133,
    142, 147
    on ablative absolute, 93–103
Anselm of Canterbury, 9, 140
Apollonius Dyscolus, 4, 7, 35, 114, 136
Aquinas, *see* Thomas Aquinas
Aristotle, 9, 41–2, 137, 143
    Categories, 8, 140
    De interpretatione, 8, 11, 28, 69, 79, 122,
        139, 140, 143–4
    Prior Analytics, 140
    Posterior Analytics, 19, 21, 64
    Physics, 45, 76–82, 144–6
    Sophistici Elenchi, 11

Bacon, Roger, 20, 23, 54, 74–6, 82
Bauer, L., 36, 59
Baum, R., 87
Bloomfield, L., 12
Blund, Robert, 19, 115, 140, 148
Boethius (sixth-century logician), 8, 15,
    136, 144
Boethius Dacus, 23, 26, 27, 31, 34–5, 85–8,
    106, 139, 146–7, 149
Bursill-Hall, G. L., 1, 48, 50, 59, 138–9

Carden, G., 102
Charisius, 4
Chomsky, N., 71

Covington, M. A., 49, 50, 140
Cracoviensis, *see* Anonymus Cracoviensis

Dacia (= Denmark), 23
D'Ailly, P., 124–5, 149
Despauterius, J., 126, 132, 149
Dialectica Monacensis, 11–12
Diomedes, 4
Doctrinale, *see* Alexander de Villa Dei
Donatus, 4, 72, 121, 128–31, 149
Duns Scotus, Johannes, 138

Ebbesen, S., 69, 137
Eberhardus Bethuniensis, 13
Enders, H. W., 24, 111–12, 139, 145
Erfurt (schools at), 120
Expositio Donati nominalis, 128–31, 149

Fernández García, M., 138
Fierville, C., 43
Fredborg, K. M., vii, 10, 21, 134, 137, 140

Gansiniec, R., 138
Garlandus Compotista, 9
Gerbert of Aurillac, 9
Goswin of Marbais, 23, 139
Grabmann, M., 134
Green-Pedersen, N. J., 134
Guarino Veronese, 132
Guido (twelfth-century grammarian), 15–16
Gundissalinus, Dominicus, 20

Helias, *see* Petrus Helias
Hockett, C. F., 7
Honorius Augustodunensis, 136
Hudson, R. A., 59
Hugh of St Victor, 13, 42, 44, 57–8, 132,
    141, 149
Hunt, R. W., 9–10, 136

Jacobi, K., 137
Jeauneau, É., 136
Johannes Aurifaber, 120–3
Johannes Dacus, 23, 34

Index of topics

ablative absolute, 13, 47
accent, 6, 136
accidens concretum, 148
accidentia, 65–6
actual (vs. potential), 41, 48–9, 77, 142–3
albus, 36, 140
allotheta, 73
ambiguity, 11
amphibologia, 11
anaphora, 58–9, 113–19, 126–7
ante, see ex parte ante/post
appositum, 69–70, 144
ars, 19
article (in Greek), 26–7, 139
astronomy, 2, 136, 144
Averroism, 120

causae inventionis, 9–10
complementarity, *see proportio*
compositio (=implicit copula), 66, 68, 79–80, 143–4
conceptio personarum, 91–2
conceptus, 31–2
concidentia, 74
concord, 13, 29–30, 35, 48, 62–8, 85, 119, 126, 149
congruitas, 33–5, 61–8, 70, 74, 121, 124–5
   secundum intellectum, 71
conjunction
   as *medium construendi*, 146–7
   as syntactic problem, 83–92, 100
consignificare, 11, 28, 30–2, 34–5
constituent structure, 36, 69–70, 83–103
constructibile, 30, 32
   primum, see primum–secundum relation
constructio, 32–40, 41, 42–4, 126
   see also principium constructionis
construction
   actuum/personarum, 37, 140
   endocentric/exocentric, 59
   reciprocal, retransitive, 8, 43, 44, 79
   transitive/intransitive, 8, 37, 42–3, 44–6, 52–6, 79, 85, 88–9, 127, 143, 146

construitur cum, 7, 16, 18
co-reference, 39, 44–6, 114–19

dédoublement, 87
dependency grammar, 59, 83, 87
dependens–terminans relation, 37, 39–40, 41, 48–51, 62, 67, 126, 140, 141, 142
dependentia, 126, 140
   mediata, 43, 52–4, 141
determinatio, 15–16, 18, 47
Diasynthetica (= *Diasyntactica*), 23, 127
dicendum est, 2, 143
dictio, 6
distantia
   physical, 77, 80
   semantic, 71–2, 80
distributional constraints, 7, 26

elementa, 6
ellipsis, 8
embedding, 93–103
et, see conjunction
Etymologia, 23, 127
ex parte ante/post, 56–7, 95–7, 103, 126, 143
exigere, exigit, exigentia, 7, 16, 18, 47, 62, 141
extremum, 77, 142

figures of construction, 72–6, 91–2
form (vs. matter), 41, 48–50, 142–3
French language, 21, 143

government, 8
   see also regimen
grammaticality, 33–4, 61–76
Greek language, 21
   definite article, 26–7, 139
   (for individual Greek terms see Index of Greek terms)
gubernare, 137

Hebrew language, 21
history of linguistics, methodology of, 2–3

INDEX OF GREEK TERMS